Lancashire
MURDERS

Lancashire
MURDERS

Alan Hayhurst

The
History
Press

First published in the United Kingdom in 2004

The History Press
97 St George's Place,
Cheltenham, Gloucestershire, GL50 3QB
www.thehistorypress.co.uk

Reprinted 2005, 2010, 2023

British Library Cataloguing in Publication Data
A catalogue record for this book is available from the British Library.

ISBN 978-0-7509-3693-4

Typeset in 10.5/13.5pt Sabon
Typesetting and origination by
The History Press.
Printed by TJ Books Limited, Padstow, Cornwall

CONTENTS

Acknowledgements   vii

Introduction   ix

1.   Steeped in Arsenic   1
   Liverpool, 1889

2.   The Body in the Wardrobe   20
   Bury, 1889

3.   Triple Murder   30
   Lancaster, 1905

4.   The Brides in the Bath   38
   Blackpool, 1913

5.   The Man from the Pru   54
   Liverpool, 1931

6.   Red Stains on the Carpet   75
     Lancaster, 1935

7.   One Death Sentence too Many   94
     Manchester, 1946

8.   Fourth Time Unlucky   107
     Southport, 1947

9.   Death at the Hospital   118
     Blackburn, 1948

10. A Poisonous Couple   130
     Blackpool, 1953

     Bibliography   144

     Index   147

ACKNOWLEDGEMENTS

The author is indebted to and would like to thank the staff of the National Archive at Kew, who were ever helpful; the staff of Blackburn, Bolton, Bury and Southport Reference Libraries; the Lancashire Family History and Heraldry Society; Miss Joan Gardner for sharing with me her memories of Dr Ruxton; Raymond Hamm for allowing me to look at his father's papers re the Griffiths case; the indefatigable James Tattersall, who helped tremendously with researches in Southport; George Barnes, Sarah Bryce, Hazel Butler; Chris Dawson of the Friends of Real Lancashire for permission to quote from his article on the real Lancashire; Bob Dobson, Cliff and Marie Elmer, Stewart Evans, Jonathan Goodman, Tracey Griffiths, Geoff Hayman, Sally Knapman, J. Roger Maltby; Kevin Mulley at Bury Archives Service; Tony Rae, Audrey Stevenson, Linda Stratmann and Richard Whittington-Egan.

I also owe a big debt of gratitude to my wife, who provided advice, proofreading and endless cups of coffee during the writing of this book and who accepted my long absences, cloistered in the office upstairs, without complaint.

INTRODUCTION

The proud county of Lancashire has a history going back to Norman times and in the centuries since then has provided the country with princes, parliamentarians, entrepreneurs, captains of industry, and the famous and unique Lancashire dialect – not forgetting also the millions of Lancastrians of both sexes who provided the labour force that worked in the cotton, coal-mining and papermaking industries, bringing wealth and prosperity to the county.

Lancashire also seems to have had more than its fair share of notorious crimes, many of which hit the national headlines. It is difficult to find a crime that is both interesting and unusual that has not been thoroughly dissected by other authors, but all those included here bear further re-examination. Wherever possible I have included new angles and viewpoints, some of which are my own, formed during forty years of research and including material from discussions with people who were living at the time the crime was committed and who were willing to give me the benefit of their recollections.

Naturally, as the most recent crime dealt with is now fifty years old, the number of people with personal knowledge is necessarily limited, but I have been surprised just how many there are who either still remember, or who have personal papers in respect of, events which are now just a distant memory to most. Less than a year ago, I was asked to give a talk to a group of partially sighted people in Liverpool, many of them elderly, and when I asked at the start whether anyone remembered the Wallace case of 1931 (see Chapter 5), a forest of hands flew up. One young man even came to me at the end of the talk and told me that he and his wife had lived in Wallace's house, 29 Wolverton Street, for a time without knowing what had taken place there. Concerning a murder that took place elsewhere in the county, I have lost count of the number of people who have sung to me the rhyme that they were taught by their mothers about the Ruxton crime; it begins, 'Red stains on the carpet' (see Chapter 6).

For much of the verbatim detail of my stories I have consulted trial transcripts and many boxes of records at the National Archives (formerly the Public Record Office) as well as newspaper reports of the time. The latter have the advantage of often dealing with the atmosphere in the courtroom and the demeanour of the personalities involved. I am also indebted to the excellent Notable British Trials series and in the Wallace case, W.F. Wyndham-Brown's account of the trial.

I have avoided putting words into the mouths of participants in the cases covered here without having seen some written evidence, such as trial transcripts, notes, letters and the like; where I have done so, or have described events that could only have been witnessed by the characters themselves, I have followed as closely as possible the recorded events of the case. For example, only Dr Ruxton knows how he dropped those grisly remains into the Gardenholme Linn, but I have checked the weather conditions at the time and know from the evidence the rough course of events, so I am confident that my description of his actions on that terrible night is as accurate as it can be.

Finally, if any of my readers protest that Manchester and Liverpool are now part of Greater Manchester and Merseyside respectively and so are no longer in Lancashire, I would remind them that these are merely administrative counties and that the traditional boundaries of Lancashire still exist. To quote the Department of the Environment, 3 September 1991: 'The Local Government Act 1972 did not abolish traditional counties, only administrative ones. Although for local government purposes some of the historic counties have ceased to be administrative areas, they continue to exist for other purposes.'

1
STEEPED IN ARSENIC

Liverpool, 1889

In the Liverpool district of Aigburth, a narrow thoroughfare runs from Aigburth Road down to Otterspool Promenade on the banks of the Mersey. To the left of the road are playing fields, including the Liverpool Cricket Club's ground, and on the right, almost hidden behind a crumbling wall running along a cracked and uneven pavement, is a large, twenty-roomed Victorian mansion, now divided into two separate properties and numbered 6 and 7 Riversdale Road. In 1889 the property was an imposing, three-storeyed house standing on its own amid extensive lawns, kitchen garden and orchards, and was known as Battlecrease House, the residence of Mr and Mrs James Maybrick.

James Maybrick was born in 1838, the third of five brothers, all of whom grew up to be successful businessmen. Although James had prospered as a cotton broker in partnership with his younger brother Edwin, the natural leader of the family was Michael Maybrick, who though not the eldest was the one to whom the family tended to turn in times of crisis. Under the pseudonym of 'Stephen Adams', Michael was a writer of popular songs, including 'The Holy City', and was fast becoming famous.

Unmarried at the age of 42, James fancied himself as a bit of a dandy: he was always immaculately turned out, sporting a gold watch chain and diamond tiepin and smoking the most luxurious cigars. Business was good; he enjoyed himself at the lavish balls that were the fashion in the 1880s and particularly at the races, including the high spot of the season, the Aintree Grand National. His business regularly took him to America and, as he was returning from such a visit in 1881 on the White Star liner Baltic, his attention was drawn to a young American girl who was travelling to England with her mother, the Baroness von Roques. Florence Elizabeth Chandler was 18 years old, a slender young woman with a long face and heavy jaw. Her hair was cut short and curled in the fashion of the day and, despite not being a classical beauty, she radiated youthful energy. It was soon clear to her fellow passengers that she had made a conquest in James Maybrick. The two of them

Florence Maybrick at about the time of her marriage. (Author's collection)

became inseparable as the voyage progressed, and as the ship approached Liverpool there were rumours in the first-class dining room of a possible engagement. However, it was impossible in the few short days they had spent together that either should get to know much about the other or the other's family; had they done so, it seems highly likely that the 'engagement' would have ended abruptly.

Florence was born in September 1862 in Mobile, Alabama. Her father died when she was very young and her mother, Caroline, married again – another union that did not last long. The third husband rejoiced in the name of Baron Adolph von Roques, a grand-sounding title although he had little money to back it up. After seven years this marriage also broke up, leaving Caroline free to travel about Europe, taking her growing daughter with her. Her son, Holbrook Chandler, was several years older than Florence and was studying for a career in medicine. Caroline von Roques was an adventuress and more than a little bohemian, but it is surprising that she allowed Florence to strike up such a serious relationship with a man old enough to be her father; one can also wonder what Florence saw in the middle-aged Maybrick other than, perhaps, his obvious wealth.

Outwardly a highly respectable merchant, Maybrick had two dark secrets that he kept hidden from the world. First, he was something of a hypochondriac, subject to frequent minor illnesses for which he dosed himself incessantly with whatever potion the local pharmacist would supply. These potions, more often than not without a doctor's prescription, contained small doses of toxic substances, usually arsenic or strychnine, and over the years the proportion of poison had increased. People introduced to him for the first time were often startled when he announced that he took enough arsenic to kill a lesser man, and they marvelled when he poured a white powder onto his food, claiming that it was arsenic to keep him virile. He also claimed that he had taken in so much arsenic over the years that he was now immune to its poisonous effects. On its own, that foible might have been bearable.

James Maybrick.
(Richard Whittington-Egan)

However, his second secret, which of course neither mother nor daughter knew, was that Florence's suitor – although unmarried – had a mistress in England who had already borne him three children and who was dependent upon him for their support. Nevertheless, the couple were married at the fashionable St James's Church, Piccadilly, on 27 July 1880 and their first child, James Chandler Maybrick, was born on 24 March the following year – only eight months after the marriage, as some of the sharper members of the Maybrick family may have muttered quietly to themselves.

During the cotton season the couple regularly commuted to and from America and, when they were home, they took an increasing part in the Liverpool social scene. In 1884 James Maybrick took the lease of Battlecrease House, where they entertained their friends to musical evenings and lavish balls; it was here that, in June 1886, their second child, Gladys Evelyn Maybrick, was born. Extra servants were taken on to cope with the increasing workload but, for whatever reason, the Maybricks did not seem to keep their servants very long and by 1889, just three years later, none of the 1886 servants was still in their employ.

In 1887 there was an outbreak of scarlatina and, as a precaution, James Maybrick took Gladys to Wales for a time, young James having already had the disease. It was during this period that Florence somehow discovered the existence of James's mistress and her children, who now numbered five, two of them having been born since Maybrick's marriage. There was a dreadful row when Florence confronted James with what she knew, and her first instinct was to go back to mother; but in the end she settled for moving into a separate bedroom – an event that was immediately noted, with disapproval, by the servants.

For the next couple of years the Maybricks presented a united front to the world and few, if any, outside Battlecrease House knew of the situation. They carried on their social whirl, attending the theatre and musical events as though nothing had happened, and they were always to be seen at the local race meetings. In the meantime James Maybrick continued to dose himself with any potion to hand, until in 1888 a worried Florence consulted her doctor about the 'strong medicine' that her husband was in the habit of taking and which he admitted always seemed to make him worse rather than better. The doctor was well aware of Maybrick's hypochondriac tendencies, and so did nothing.

A local chemist, Edwin Heaton, had for years been supplying Maybrick with a potion of Maybrick's own devising that called for 'four drops of liquor arsenicalis'. He now noticed that his client had increased the arsenic to seven drops and that he was an ever more frequent visitor to the shop, sometimes coming in for his 'special' draught several times a day. In addition, James always made sure that he had a good supply to hand when he went out of town.

Later that year, the Maybricks were introduced to a wealthy cotton merchant, the 38-year-old Alfred Brierley: a handsome, bearded man. The three hit it off immediately and before long Brierley was a regular visitor to Battlecrease House. As he also had an interest in horse racing, it was soon rare for the Maybricks to attend any function where Brierley was not also present. It is not clear exactly when the relationship between Alfred Brierley and Florence turned into something more than formal friendship, but in the spring of 1889 Florence announced to her husband that she would be spending a few days in London with an aunt who was recovering from an operation. On Friday 21 March Florence arrived at Flatman's Hotel in Cavendish Square, where rooms had been booked in the names of Mr and Mrs Thomas Maybrick, and she was followed some hours later by Brierley. The couple tended to stay in their room and had most of their meals sent up, but after only three days Brierley left the hotel and Florence moved on to visit the home of her cousin. She also had dinner with Michael Maybrick, before returning to Liverpool on 29 March.

On the Saturday the Aintree Grand National was held, a very special occasion as the Prince of Wales and his retinue were present and everybody who was anybody in local society attended – including the Maybricks. To

Battlecrease House. (Author)

no one's surprise, Alfred Brierley appeared as well and attached himself to Maybrick's party. Everyone cheered when the amateur jockey Mr Beasley rode Frigate to the winning post. Then, in front of James and his party, Brierley made a point of asking Florence to accompany him to see the Prince of Wales and she agreed eagerly. She took his arm and the couple walked off, leaving Maybrick plainly discomfited. By the time Florence returned, he was in a towering rage and complaining that the whole of Liverpool society had noticed his wife walking arm in arm with a man who was not her husband. In silence, the couple returned to Battlecrease House, where the servants instantly detected that something was wrong.

Alice Yapp had been the children's nurse at Battlecrease House for nearly two years and she and the other four servants regarded their mistress with ill-concealed dislike, being of the opinion that she was an American gold-digger who had tricked their master into marriage. When the Maybricks returned from the races they went into the nursery together and Yapp hastened to put her ear to the door, just in time to hear James say to his wife, 'This scandal will be all over the town tomorrow, Florrie. I never thought you could come to this.' A few minutes later James ordered a servant to call a cab, but when Florence moved towards the front door he shouted at her, 'If you once cross this threshold, you shall never enter these doors again.' Nurse Yapp went to comfort her mistress, noting that she had the beginnings of a black eye, and James fell exhausted onto the settle in the hall.

Florence by now had had enough and decided to seek a separation from her husband, whom she knew was still seeing his mistress on a regular basis. James's four brothers showed her little sympathy and so she consulted a physician, Dr Hopper, who promised to have a word with her husband; but there was a problem. Unknown to James, Florence was heavily in debt and Hopper suggested that she should make a clean breast of it in an effort to start all over again. Florence followed his advice. To her surprise, James took the confession calmly and even promised to settle the debts for her. Unfortunately, this reunion did not last long and soon the couple were arguing again. James now insisted on seeing Florence's mail before the maid took it up to her room and on several occasions returned letters to the sender, unread. He continued to take the usual mixture of potions and complained to his brother Michael of persistent pains in the head and numbness in his limbs, which Michael suggested to him might have something to do with the medicines he was taking. James angrily refused to accept this diagnosis.

Towards the end of April, Florence visited the shop of Mr Thomas Symington Wokes in Aigburth, who gave evidence at the later trial that she had asked for a supply of flypapers. It was, perhaps, a little early in the year to be troubled by flies, but Wokes supplied a dozen willingly. The papers were about six inches square, impregnated with arsenic and were meant to be placed in a saucerful of water, so that the resulting solution poisoned any insect that drank it. It was a medium-term solution to the fly problem, as they took some time to die, but the papers were very popular and sold in their thousands.

At about the same time, Maybrick consulted his solicitor with a view to remaking his will. He proposed appointing his brothers Michael and Thomas to be his executors and left the greater part of his estate in trust for the benefit of his children, including all his furniture. Florence was to have the proceeds of two life policies totalling £2,500 – which were in her name anyway and strictly not in James's gift – and she was to be allowed to remain at Battlecrease House with the children for so long as she remained a widow. The will was an ill-thought-out document, somewhat hastily drawn up and leaving Florence the bare minimum on which to survive should her husband predecease her. In addition to her own private income from America of £120 per annum, the investment proceeds of the life policies were unlikely to bring in much more than £200 a year, the combined sum being insufficient for the upkeep of Battlecrease House, let alone the support of the children and Florence herself. It might therefore be necessary for Florence to throw herself on the mercy of the executors, something that she was uncomfortably aware she could not rely upon.

Bottles containing various liquids continued to be delivered by post and Florence confided to the servants that some of them contained strychnine. One day Maybrick appeared at his office complaining of numbness in the lower limbs and told friends that he had taken an overdose of strychnine that morning. The following day Nurse Yapp, having been summoned by Florence, found James lying on the bed in some distress and was sent to ask the cook for a draught of mustard and water, as 'James has taken another dose of that horrid medicine.' Dr Humphreys was called and Florence mentioned to him the white powder that her husband was in the habit of taking, but when questioned by the doctor about it, Maybrick dismissed this as the cause of his ill health. Humphreys, used to Maybrick's hypochondriac ways, remained unconcerned and merely prepared a diet sheet. Edwin Maybrick called to see his brother and stayed for a few days until James declared himself better and returned to work. That evening he accompanied his wife to a grand masked ball, which they both seem to have enjoyed.

Early in May, James again complained of feeling unwell and Dr Humphreys prescribed Valentine's Meat Juice, prussic acid and a mouthwash of Condy's Fluid; on 6 May the prescription was changed to Fowler's Solution of Arsenic, a popular pick-me-up of the time containing arsenic, carbonate of potash and lavender water. Later, at the trial, Dr Humphreys would say that the whole bottle of Fowler's Solution contained only about one twenty-fifth of a grain of arsenic. The usual minimum fatal dose of arsenic is two grains, and so drinking the whole of the bottle of Fowler's at one go would not necessarily have caused Maybrick anything other than a slight stomach upset. However, combined with all the other potions that he was in the habit of taking, and bearing in mind that arsenic can also have a cumulative effect, building up in the body and particularly in the liver and kidneys over a period of time until quite a small additional dose is lethal, it could not have helped his condition.

On the same day, 6 May, Alfred Brierley wrote a letter to Florence, worried that James Maybrick knew something about their stay in London and telling her that he proposed to leave the area for a while, not coming back until the autumn when things might have quietened down.

On 7 May Edwin Maybrick received a telegram from Florence asking him to send a doctor to examine his brother, who was no better, and that afternoon a Dr Carter arrived at Battlecrease House, having been sent for because of his reputation in the locality. He was followed shortly after by Dr Humphreys. Together they examined James, who was vomiting copiously and, rather surprisingly, they decided that he was on the mend and thought that he might well recover within a few days. No attempt was made to discover the cause of his illness, although given the state of medical science at the time and the almost medieval treatment that he had been subjected to, that is not to be wondered at. A former girlfriend of Maybrick, Matilda Jannion, by now Mrs Briggs, called at the house accompanied by her sister Martha, now Mrs Hughes. They had been asked to call by Michael Maybrick and, despite the fact that they had no business being there, the sisters insisted that James should have a qualified nurse, whom Florence reluctantly agreed to pay for.

The next day Nurse Ellen Ann Gore arrived and took over the management of the patient, noting that James was plainly unwell and constantly complaining that he felt as though he had a hair tickling his throat. She and her relief, Nurse Callery, watched over James and gave him various mixtures, including a few drops of Valentine's Meat Juice which had been brought by Edwin Maybrick. On the evening of 9 May Nurse Gore noticed Florence go into James's bedroom and take out of a drawer the partly used bottle of Valentine's, which she took into the dressing room, remaining there with the door closed for a short time. On returning she placed the bottle of meat juice back on the bedside table and told the nurse to fetch some ice to put in water, so that she could bathe her husband's head. Meanwhile, the rather appropriately named Alice Yapp had approached the Jannion sisters and confided, 'The mistress is poisoning the master.' She told them about the flypapers that she had seen soaking and implied that this was something sinister, although countless thousands of such fly killers were even then being soaked in houses the length and breadth of the country, as no doubt the three of them knew very well.

That afternoon Michael Maybrick received a telegram from Mrs Briggs saying, 'Come at once. Strange things going on here', while at about the same time Florence sat down to write a letter to Alfred Brierley. He was the only person she felt she could turn to in what was becoming an increasingly antagonistic household. Finishing the letter, she sealed it and gave it to Alice Yapp to post, perhaps in her distress failing to see the risk she was taking in involving the servant in her intrigue. Yapp later claimed that she had given the letter to baby Gladys to carry on her walk to the post office and that the baby had dropped it into a puddle. Yapp found a clean envelope and as she was putting the letter in it, she 'inadvertently read some of the contents' and decided to inform Edwin. The letter read as follows:

Dearest,
Your letter under cover to John K. came to hand just after I had written to you on Monday. I did not expect to hear from you so soon and had delayed in giving him the necessary instructions. Since my return, I have been nursing M day and night. *He is sick unto death.* The doctors held a consultation today and now all depends upon how long his strength will hold out! Both my brothers-in-law are here and we are terribly anxious. I cannot answer your letter fully today, my darling, but relieve your mind of all fear of discovery now and in the future. M has been delirious since Sunday and I know now that he is perfectly ignorant of everything, even to the name of the street, and also that he has not been making any enquiries whatever. The tale he told me was pure fabrication and only intended to frighten the truth out of me. In fact, he believes my statement, although he will not admit it. You need not go abroad on that account, dearest, but in any case please don't leave England until I have seen you once again. You must feel that these two letters of mine were written under circumstances that must even excuse their injustice in your eyes. Do you suppose I could act as I am doing if I really felt and meant what I inferred then? If you wish to write to me about anything, do so now, as all the letters pass through my hands at present. Excuse this scrawl, my own darling, but I dare not leave the room for a moment and I do not know when I shall be able to write to you again.

Yours in haste,
Florrie.

Florence's letter, admitting her illicit relationship with Brierley and appearing to forecast the death of her husband ('he is sick unto death'), was somewhat ill advised and largely responsible for the verdict at her subsequent trial. Edwin and Michael Maybrick arrived that evening, having had the chance to discuss the letter on the way from the station and Michael Maybrick was in no doubt. 'The woman is an adulteress,' he said savagely to his brother. They immediately confronted Florence and made plain their suspicions. Michael led the onslaught and insisted that she was not looking after James properly and that his brother should have had the services of a professional nurse much earlier in his illness. The facts that James had consulted several doctors in the recent past, all of whom had thought that there was little wrong with him except stomach ache and hypochondria, and that it was Florence who had contacted Edwin on 7 May asking for his help, seem to have escaped him. The brothers insisted that all food and medicine was henceforth to be handled by Nurse Gore and no one else.

Later, Michael Maybrick went to the house of Dr Humphreys and discussed his brother's prospects. The doctor, ignoring medical ethics regarding the confidentiality of his patient's affairs, said that James had told him that he was going to die, whereupon Michael Maybrick told him about the flypapers and Alice Yapp's suspicions, before returning to Battlecrease House determined to watch even more closely over his ailing brother. The next day Nurse Callery arrived to relieve the exhausted Nurse Gore, and found her patient weak and complaining of a burning sensation in his throat and pains in the abdomen.

On that same day, Friday 9 May, there was another visit from Drs Carter and Humphreys, during which Michael Maybrick demanded to know what was wrong with his brother. 'Dyspepsia,' was the reply. 'I am aware of that,' said Michael angrily. 'But what is causing it?' Both doctors admitted that they did not know, but suspected that it was something that James had taken in with his food. Michael remarked that his brother had been ill on and off for the past month, having had several vomiting fits, and that he seemed better when away from home. This was a lie, as James had rarely ventured out since the beginning of his illness and had not spent a single night away from Battlecrease House. Michael also told the doctors that James was estranged from his wife, who had recently been buying flypapers about which there was the 'gravest suspicion'. Armed with this information the doctors re-examined their patient and, having now decided that his symptoms could have been caused by poison, took samples for analysis. The result was negative, and the following day Nurse Gore returned to duty and prepared a dose of Valentine's Meat Juice for the invalid, despite Florence's complaint that the juice had made her husband sick on other occasions when he had taken it. By this time, in response to Michael Maybrick's instructions, the servants were taking little notice of what their mistress said, ignoring the fact that she was the only person, apart from her husband, who had any legal standing in the house.

James became worse and when Nurse Callery came on duty, Nurse Gore told her about the incident with the meat juice, whereupon Callery took a clean bottle and poured some of the remaining liquid into it. On her way out, Gore told Michael Maybrick that she was not happy about a half-bottle of brandy in James's room and so Maybrick commandeered it. It was obvious that a nervous panic was beginning to sweep through the house, affecting principals and servants alike. Later, Michael Maybrick caught Florence decanting medicine from one bottle to another and angrily accused her of meddling. Florence protested that there was so much sediment in the medicine that she was pouring it into a larger bottle so that it could be shaken more easily, but when Dr Humphreys arrived on his rounds Maybrick handed him the meat juice and the brandy and asked him to have them analysed.

James's treatment continued, including a nutrient suppository and sulphonal, a sleep-inducing drug, but he grew steadily weaker. The following morning the doctor arrived at around 8.30 to find the Jannion sisters in attendance, having apparently been sent for by Florence. James was obviously dying and his wife was lying on her bed, semi-comatose and exhausted. The previous evening Dr Humphreys had carried out tests on the two bottles that he had been given; the brandy proved to be innocuous, but the meat juice tested positive for arsenic. When Dr Carter arrived at noon, Humphreys gave him this information and Carter decided to hold on to the bottle for the time being. 'In the event of James's death,' he said, 'I will be unable to sign a death certificate until the bottle has been examined by a skilled analyst.'

James Maybrick breathed his last at 8.40 that evening, with his wife still unconscious in the next room. Michael immediately gave orders that the house was to be vacated and that the servants were to search the property to see what they could find. Alice Yapp began to put some of the children's clothes in a trunk and discovered a chocolate box containing a small parcel wrapped in brown paper. In it were a packet and two bottles, the packet bearing the words 'Poison', 'Arsenic' and 'Poison for cats'. The bottles contained a white fluid. A solicitor, Mr A.G. Steel, lived next door and his advice was sought by Michael Maybrick: Steel judged that anything that might be evidence should be sealed and kept for the authorities. Maybrick immediately made a parcel of the chocolate box and contents, which he sealed and locked in the wine cellar.

By Sunday morning, 12 May, Florence had recovered somewhat, to find that the servants were whispering among themselves about poison and that a search of the house was taking place in case further amounts could be found. Michael Maybrick was looking for James's will, which could not be located; and the servants had been told that Florence was no longer in charge of the household and that Michael and Edwin would take all decisions until further notice. Mrs Briggs joined in the poison search and it was she who discovered two gentlemen's hatboxes in Florence's bedroom, one of which contained several small bottles, including a bottle of Valentine's. In the other was a tumbler containing a clear liquid in which a piece of cloth was soaking.

The children were taken off to the home of Mrs Jannion, mother of Mrs Briggs and Mrs Hughes, and as they left Michael Maybrick told the nurse who was looking after Florence that 'Mrs Maybrick is no longer mistress of this house and, as one of the executors, I forbid you to allow her to leave this room.' Michael Maybrick had absolutely no authority to give such an order, but the nurse could not be expected to know that and so Florence was now virtually a prisoner in her own home.

The police were informed of the suspicious death of James Maybrick and they arrived at Battlecrease House to interview the servants. Inspector Baxendale took charge of the hatboxes and contents and some other items, the packet from the chocolate box being handed to the police by Michael Maybrick the following day when he returned from a visit to London. The post-mortem examination was performed by Drs Humphreys and Carter, watched by Dr Alexander Baron, Professor of Pathology at University College, together with Police Superintendent Bryning. Dr Baron's opinion was that death was due to acute inflammation of the stomach, probably caused by an irritant poison; and on Tuesday 14 May, at the Aigburth Hotel, an inquest was opened which was promptly adjourned for fourteen days to allow further tests to be carried out. Florence now obtained the services of solicitors Cleaver and Arnold to watch over her interests, which was just as well, as later that day she was arrested on suspicion of causing the death of her husband.

Florence told her lawyers that early on Thursday evening James had asked her to give him a powder, which he was in the habit of taking. At first she had declined, but her husband was so insistent that she eventually gave in and put the powder in the meat juice. Only now, she said, did she realise that the powder was white arsenic. She had also written another letter to Alfred Brierley:

I am writing you to give me every assistance in your power in my present fearful trouble. I am in custody, without any of my family with me and without money. I have cabled my solicitor in New York to come here at once. In the meantime, send me money for present needs. The truth is known about my visit to London. Your last letter is at present in the hands of the police. Appearances may be against me, but before God, I swear I am innocent.

Florence, who did not appear to have learned her lesson, handed the letter to Mrs Briggs, who in turn handed it straight over to the police.

On Wednesday 15 May the story hit the newspapers, the headline in the Liverpool Daily Post proclaiming, 'The Maybrick Mystery'. The following day, still at home under the vigilant eyes of the nurses and the duty policemen, a distraught Florence watched from an upstairs window as her husband's coffin left for the funeral, which the police did not permit her to attend.

A local tailor called at the house to present a bill for ladies' dresses, none of which, Florence said, was anything to do with her. The tailor confirmed that they had not been made for Mrs Maybrick, but as James Maybrick had had dresses made for the lady in question on other occasions, he expected that Maybrick's executors would honour the bill for £10!

A search of James's office disclosed nearly thirty bottles and pillboxes, some of which were locked up in his private desk. Another seven bottles of pills had been found at Battlecrease House, and Nurse Yapp produced a further twenty-eight items of medicine. Fifty-one items came from Maybrick's dressing room – some marked 'poison' – and in the lavatory were another twenty-four bottles, ointments and powders. Altogether the police took away more than 160 items, and at that point the decision was made to have Florence taken from Battlecrease House to Liverpool (Walton) Prison.

The inquest was reopened and the notorious 'sick unto death' letter was read out in open court. Maybrick's body had been exhumed and specimens taken for examination, but only minute quantities of arsenic were found, insufficient to have caused his death. Evidence was given as to the deceased's liking for arsenic potions and Dr Humphreys was forced to admit that he himself had prescribed Fowler's solution.

The foreman of the jury resigned after writing to the coroner that he knew James Maybrick and had heard him talking about taking doses of arsenic, but this information was kept from the court. The verdict of the coroner's jury was 'death resulting from an irritant poison' and, by a majority of thirteen to one, that it had been administered by Florence Maybrick. Florence was committed to the next assizes on a charge of murder.*

The trial opened in the imposing surroundings of St George's Hall, Liverpool, with Sir James Fitzjames Stephen presiding. John Addison QC, MP, appeared with Messrs W.R. McConnell and Thomas Swift for the prosecution, while appearing for Florence were the redoubtable Sir Charles Russell QC, MP, and Mr William Pickford. Addison started by recounting James Maybrick's courtship and marriage and also the nature of James's hypochondriac disposition. He mentioned the trouble at the races and Florence's few days in London with Alfred Brierley, which brought gasps from the public gallery and made the reporters in the press box scribble furiously in their notebooks.

---

* Until as late as 1978, a coroner's jury had, among their duties, to ascertain the person or persons to be charged with murder, manslaughter, infanticide or with being accessories before the fact in cases where the jury might find that the deceased came by his death by murder, manslaughter or infanticide. The Broderick Committee, in 1976, reporting on death certification and coroners, recommended that the coroner should no longer have the power to commit a named person for trial. Lord Lucan, wanted for the murder of Sandra Rivett, was the last person to be named by a coroner's inquest, in June 1975.

St George's Hall, Liverpool, scene of many trials, including those of Maybrick and Wallace (see Chapter 5). (Author's collection)

It was evident that the first prosecution witness, Michael Maybrick, was hostile to the accused, being definite whenever he had something to say which was against Florence and vague about anything that might have been in her favour. He claimed not to recall his brother ever having complained about ill health or having dosed himself except, he told the court, a mention of this in a letter from Florence, which he had thrown away. He did, however, agree that she had referred to a white powder that she had seen her husband take on several occasions, and that she claimed to have looked for poison but had not found any.

A parade of medical men then gave evidence. Dr Thomas Stevenson, who stated that he had many years' experience as a toxicologist, said that he had found an *almost* fatal dose of arsenic in the samples he had been sent for analysis; and Dr William Carter opined that Maybrick's death had been caused by acute arsenical poisoning, the poison having been administered on Friday 3 May, although he could give no cogent reason as to why he picked that particular day. He also had to admit under cross-examination that he had never before had a patient who had died from arsenical poisoning. Dr Arthur Hopper confirmed that Maybrick was a hypochondriac who tended to attach undue importance to his symptoms, and he agreed that Florence had mentioned that her husband was in the habit of taking a very strong medicine, which had a bad influence on him. Dr Fuller described his examination of James Maybrick on 14 April at Michael Maybrick's request. He had been of the opinion that there was little wrong with James apart from indigestion, and he had seen no indication that Maybrick was in the habit of taking arsenic.

Dr Richard Humphreys admitted that he might not have carried out the test for arsenic properly, as he was not skilled in making such a test. He also found it impossible to distinguish between the symptoms of arsenical poisoning and gastro-enteritis and, but for information given to him by Michael Maybrick, he would have signed the death certificate certifying that James had died from gastritis. At various times, James Maybrick had been treated with cascara (a laxative), nitro-hydrochloric acid, nux vomica, phosphorus pills, potassium bromide (an anti-convulsant), Fowler's Solution

The holding cell immediately underneath the dock of Liverpool Crown Court, where both Florence Maybrick and William Wallace (see Chapter 5) awaited the jury's verdict. (Author)

of Arsenic, tincture of hyoscyamus (for intestinal cramps and diarrhoea), antipyrin, tincture of jaborandi (given to induce sweating and to promote the flow of saliva), chlorine, morphia, bismuth and an opium suppository, as well as cocaine and sulphonal (a sleeping draught).

The housemaid, Mary Cadwallader, told the court that James Maybrick had said to her that he had taken an overdose of the 'London Medicine' and she also implied that, by the time of James's last illness, the staff were becoming increasingly truculent and were disobeying Florence's orders. Elizabeth Humphreys, the cook, said in court that she had asked to see Mr Maybrick and Florence had refused, but despite this she 'followed in without permission'.

Then came Edward Davies, who testified that arsenic had been found as follows: in the bottle of Valentine's Meat Juice (probably added in solution), and in the intestines and liver, but not in the stomach or spleen. The handkerchief in the tumbler of liquid contained a massive 30 to 40 grains of the poison and the bottle found in the hatbox contained 12 to 15 grains of solid arsenic, with another bottle containing about the same. The packet marked 'Arsenic for cats' contained 65 grains and a bottle labelled 'The Mixture' had in it a very weak solution of arsenic. In Maybrick's office was a bottle containing nitroglycerine and about two-thirds of a grain of arsenic. There were traces in the pocket of Mrs Maybrick's dressing gown, and the flypapers contained on average 2.5 grains each. Altogether, it was clear to everyone in the court that Battlecrease House was soaked in arsenic, the total amount of which would have been enough to kill fifty people.

The law at the time did not permit the accused to give evidence on oath, but Florence was allowed to make a statement, about which the judge was careful to advise the court she could not be questioned. Florence explained the use of the flypapers by saying that she had for many years been using a face-wash which consisted mainly of arsenic, tincture of benzoin and elderflower water and it was for that reason she had purchased the flypapers and had left them soaking – to liberate the arsenic. She described how on 9 May James had begged her to give him some of his 'white powder' and after first refusing, she had given in, Maybrick having assured her that the powder could not harm him. In doing so she had knocked over the bottle of meat juice, which she then topped up with water. This was the bottle of which Michael Maybrick later took possession.

Florence's defence, led by Sir Charles Russell QC, MP, put up a spirited fight, underlining the undoubted fact that James Maybrick had been in the habit of taking numerous potions containing arsenic and that he was experienced enough to know the risk he was taking in so doing. Dr Charles Meymott Tidy claimed that the small amount of arsenic found in the body was more consistent with the regular intake of small doses than with the administration of one murderous dose and that death was almost certainly due to gastro-enteritis and not poison. Most importantly of all, apart from the purchase of flypapers there was no evidence whatsoever that Florence had bought, or had even tried to buy, any of the dozens of grains of the poison found in the house and in the many bottles discovered at Maybrick's office.

A former servant of James Maybrick, Thomas Stansell, testified that for several years before his marriage Maybrick had regularly sent him out to buy arsenic, which he would put into beef tea and drink. Various druggists then gave evidence of the supply of arsenic draughts to Maybrick and, after summing up by both counsel, Mr Justice Stephen began his own address to the jury on Tuesday 6 August. It soon became apparent that his grasp of detail was not as keen as it might have been and he testily upbraided Florence's junior counsel, William Pickford, when he corrected the judge on a matter of date. 'There is no use in disputing about whether I used one word or another,' he told him, having just described the purchase of flypapers as being in March instead of April. This was not the only occasion when counsel interrupted to correct inaccuracies in the judge's summing up, although the general impression was one of impartiality and fairness. He pointed out that Michael Maybrick had no real cause to doubt the efficiency of James's care, with a nurse being appointed and two doctors called in, and that he showed some ill feeling towards his sister-in-law from the first. It was also clear, the judge said, that James Maybrick was in the habit of dosing himself, but would fly into a temper if anyone mentioned it to him.

At four o'clock the judge suspended his summing up until the following morning, when he immediately resumed his analysis of the medical evidence, reminding the jury of Dr Stevenson's finding that there was nearly a fatal dose of arsenic in Maybrick's remains – whereas Dr Tidy said that there was not. Soon after this, however, the tenor of his remarks changed and he began putting words into the mouth of Mr Addison, who protested, to no avail. The judge then turned to the admitted adulterous relationship between Florence and Alfred Brierley and further confused the issue by referring to an unknown man who had visited Florence at Flatman's Hotel when she first arrived there. This, in fact, was an old family friend who could easily have been produced in court to prove the innocence of the matter, but the fact of the visit remained with the jury and might well have given them the opinion that Florence was even more abandoned than had already been disclosed.

Dealing with the 'sick unto death' letter, the judge pointed out that Maybrick was certainly not expected to die at that time, but Sir James Stephen did not try to disguise the disgust that he felt when reading out the infamous document. This must certainly have had a great effect on the jury, coming as it did right at the end of his summing up. The jury retired at 3.18 p.m. and only thirty-five minutes later returned with a verdict of 'Guilty'. Florence was thereupon sentenced to death, after saying that apart

THE MAYBRICK CASE.

WILL THE HOME SECRETARY ANSWER THE PRAYERS OF AN INNOCENT, THOUGH MISGUIDED WOMAN?

Cartoon campaigning for Florence Maybrick's release, c. 1900. (Alan Elmer)

from her admitted intimacy with Brierley, she was innocent. The execution was set for 26 August 1889, but the Home Secretary reviewed the case after enormous public reaction to the sentence. Papers in the National Archives show that he eventually decided that there was a small doubt about whether Maybrick had in fact died from arsenical poisoning or some other cause, and the sentence therefore would be commuted to life imprisonment. This decision suggested that there was 'reasonable doubt' as to Florence's guilt and she should therefore have been given the benefit of it and released. Unfortunately the Court of Appeal was not set up until 1907, too late for Florence, and despite the efforts of those who believed in her innocence she served a total of fifteen years' imprisonment before being released on parole in 1904. She returned to the United States and died on 23 October 1941 in a tumbledown, neglected shack in Connecticut, surrounded by her dozens of cats.

Over a hundred years after James died, it seems clear that Florence Maybrick received a raw deal. It was symptomatic of the times that much was made of her adultery, whereas that of James Maybrick was glossed over. The arsenic found in James's body was not sufficient to have killed him, and there was ample evidence of his having taking the poison in some quantity, entirely voluntarily, over a long period. Battlecrease House had contained massive quantities of the poison, none of which – apart from the flypapers – could Florence be proved to have purchased. It is almost certain that had the case come to the courts at a later date, and with a more able judge (Mr Justice Stephen suffered a stroke less than two years after the trial and died two years after that in a mental home), she would have been found not guilty, having been given the benefit of the doubt to which she was surely entitled.

There is an interesting postscript to this story. In 1992 the publishing world was astounded to hear rumours of a book, signed by the Whitechapel serial killer of 1888, 'Jack the Ripper', which was said to have been written by none other than James Maybrick himself. The book was in the form of a diary, which had been acquired under mysterious circumstances by a Liverpool artisan named Michael Barrett, and there were hints that it had been found during renovations at Battlecrease House. The discovery caused a great furore among the many people who even today still research the Whitechapel killings. Their opinion was sharply divided, some considering the diary fraudulent, others insisting that at long last the true identity of Jack the Ripper was known. The matter rumbled on for several years, although it is now generally thought that the diary is a fake. In 1998 delegates at the International Investigative Psychology Conference in Liverpool considered whether or not the diary was indeed a forgery. The delegates concluded, on a show of hands, that whoever wrote it had a disturbed mind.

2

THE BODY IN THE WARDROBE

Bury, 1889

The town of Bury is the birthplace of Sir Robert Peel, former Prime Minister and founder of the Metropolitan Police, and is also noted for papermaking and its famous Bury black puddings. It has been, by and large, a law-abiding community, although it did experience an outbreak of loom-breaking in 1826 when the cotton weavers protested about the new-fangled power looms that were taking away their livelihood. The town has been little troubled by murder and so the impact of the headlines in the Bury Times on 28 September 1889 was sensational. 'Horrible Tragedy in Bury', screamed the newsprint: 'Discovery of the Body in a Wardrobe', 'Extraordinary Case!'

No. 39 Bolton Street consisted of shop premises and a warehouse on the ground floor, with living accommodation above. It was occupied by the Gordon Furnishing Company of Manchester, which was owned by Mr Samuel Gordon and his two sons, Meyer and George, all of whom were of the Hebrew faith and considered to be very devout. Their shop manager, a former solicitor's clerk aged about 27, was William Dukes, who until a few weeks previously, had occupied the upstairs rooms with his wife. Dukes had decided to leave the accommodation provided by his employers and had taken a property about half a mile away, on the corner of North Street and Paradise Street, where his wife opened a small confectionery shop. The buying and selling of furniture was part of his duties, and it was the practice of his employers for one of them to visit the shop, usually once a month, to examine the books and check the accounting. There had been no visit for five or six weeks because Dukes had repeatedly asked the Gordons to delay the inspection because he had a customer who was planning to spend the considerable sum of £60 to £70 on furniture in the very near future. This customer was said to be trying to make up her mind whether to purchase the goods at the Bury shop or go to the Gordons' main business premises in Manchester, where the stock was much larger, so for several weeks past

Dukes had been sending messages to Manchester that this customer was due to appear on the 'following Tuesday'. Eventually, as the weeks went by and no customer appeared, Samuel Gordon decided that they would wait no longer and Dukes was told that Mr George Gordon would call at the shop on 25 September 1889.

When Gordon arrived at around nine o'clock in the morning, Dukes was nowhere to be found and the shop boy, a lad named Tootill, could give no information as to his whereabouts. Gordon went to the shop next door and in the course of conversation confided to the owner that he was determined not to leave Bury until he had seen Dukes and obtained from him a satisfactory

Site of Gordon's shop, Bolton Street, Bury (demolished c. 1970), where George Gordon was cruelly battered to death and his body hidden in a wardrobe. No. 39 is the second shop from the left. (Bury Archive Service, B00496)

explanation regarding certain matters, the nature of which he did not wish to divulge. It was the day of the Jewish New Year and, as Dukes had still not arrived by 10.30, Gordon went back to Manchester to take part in a religious ceremony. He returned in the early afternoon to find Dukes still missing. Gordon, who was becoming annoyed at the absence of his employee, waited until 1.45, when Dukes suddenly appeared and the two men immediately began an animated conversation. Dukes noticed that Tootill was in the shop and broke off to give the boy hurried instructions to obtain the services of a carter and take some furniture to 'Lime Tree House' in Prestwich, a few miles away. Tootill did as he was told, but came back later, as he had not been able to find the address that Dukes had given him. Dukes, who now appeared to be in the shop on his own, told the boy to go out and buy several articles including a padlock, which he later put on a wardrobe in the upstairs room. Tootill then helped Dukes to move this wardrobe into the warehouse at the back of the shop, after which he was given permission to go home, Dukes saying that he would be going to the theatre that evening.

Meanwhile, back in Manchester, Samuel Gordon was growing more and more agitated as the hours went by and his son George did not return home from the shop. It was important to the devout family that they should all be together on this religious occasion, and Samuel told the manager of his Burnley shop, Fabian Goldstone – who was spending the festival with them – that 'If George had been alive, he would have returned by now.'

At about 7.30, Samuel Gordon went to the Manchester Detective Office to see if they could do anything about his missing son; in the meantime, Goldstone made the trip to Bury where he encountered Dukes, who was still at the shop. When questioned, Dukes said that George had gone to Burnley with a man and a woman and that before he left he had given him a telegram to dispatch, telling his father that he would not return until Thursday morning. Goldstone, who had left it too late to get back to Manchester that evening, stayed in Bury overnight and returned to Manchester on the Thursday morning; but before leaving, he had another conversation with Dukes, who told him that George Gordon had been worried a good deal lately. Arriving back at the Manchester shop he learned that Samuel Gordon and his other son had found a telegram at their Salford warehouse, purporting to have been sent by George and explaining his absence. Goldstone confirmed that Dukes had told him that this telegram had been sent at George's request and suggested that the police would soon be able to tell if the telegram was in George's handwriting.

Samuel and Meyer Gordon were by now in a state of high alarm, as they knew that George would have had no reason to go to Burnley, especially on such a night. Hastening to Bury, they confronted Dukes at the shop and insisted that he accompany them to the police station, where they saw

Lord Nelson Hotel, Bolton Street, Bury (demolished c. 1970), where William Dukes sought solace in drink while his employer waited impatiently only five doors away. (Bury Archive Service, B00493)

Superintendent Henderson. Meyer Gordon told the superintendent that they were extremely concerned about the missing brother, as, being a devout Jew, it was unthinkable that he would not have wanted to be with his family on the occasion of the sacred festival. 'I want my brother,' he exclaimed to the policeman, as his father stood wringing his hands while Dukes, appearing to be completely unconcerned, stood by his side saying nothing. Samuel Gordon, in a state of semi-collapse, sank into a chair sobbing as Henderson instructed Sergeant Ross and Constables McLellan and Bremner to go to the shop and have a good look round. Meyer Gordon and Dukes went with them. At this stage the superintendent was far from convinced that anything had happened to George Gordon, but he felt that he had to do something to calm down the agitated father.

When the five men arrived at the shop, their initial search turned up nothing suspicious until PC Bremner went down into the cellar and found that some of the flagstones forming the floor had been lifted and replaced. Removing a few of them, he saw that the soil underneath showed signs of having been disturbed, but before he could probe further Meyer Gordon called from the back warehouse and pointed to a wardrobe, about 5ft high, that was lying on the floor in the middle of the room. The double doors were padlocked and he asked Dukes what it was doing there. Dukes explained that a Mrs Shorrocks of Rochdale had bought it and that the carter was even now waiting outside to take it there. He claimed that the buyer had placed a quantity of clothing inside, locked the doors and taken the key away with her.

Meyer, who was beginning to show signs of hysteria, now insisted that the wardrobe be opened and said that if no key could be found, he would break open the doors himself. Dukes shrugged his shoulders and made no reply, so the distraught Gordon immediately launched an attack on the doors with a piece of metal rod that was lying on the floor. In less than a minute, the wardrobe splintered open and the five men clustering round saw a bundle wrapped in a quantity of packing and an old hearthrug. Inside, lying face downwards, was the bloodstained body of George Gordon, his corpse stiff and cold and obviously having been dead for some hours. The head and neck were a mass of wounds and coagulated blood, and the right eye appeared to have been gouged out. Next to the body was a peculiarly shaped hammer, weighing about 8lb, of the sort commonly used by quarrymen or miners. The hammer was heavily bloodstained and with it the policemen found a large chisel, about 15in long. From the appearance of the head of the deceased man, it looked as though the wounds had been made by the hammer, possibly as he was sitting down to examine the account books. Sergeant Ross made a hurried examination of the shop manager. He found no blood on his person, although there were signs that Dukes had been trying to burn some of the dead man's clothing. Meyer flung himself at Dukes, shouting 'So you have murdered my brother', but was restrained, with some difficulty, by the three policemen. 'It's not me that has done that,' Dukes exclaimed, but he was immediately arrested and taken to the police station, where he was charged with the murder of George Gordon and locked up. Samuel and his son returned to Manchester, deeply affected by events.

The accused man was committed to the Manchester Winter Assizes, and the date of the trial was fixed for Thursday 28 November 1889 to enable the Jewish witnesses to give their evidence before the Sabbath. (The court had been told that the relatives of the murdered man were Jews of an exceedingly strict order and that it would be extremely distressing for them if they were to be kept in the court after six o'clock on the Friday evening.) However, on the day before the trial was due to start the Home Secretary intervened and it was made known that Dukes might have to be called to give evidence at Liverpool in the case of a warder at Strangeways prison who was accused of the manslaughter of a prisoner. Ultimately Dukes's evidence was not required in Liverpool after all his trial eventually started on Wednesday 4 December at Manchester, Mr Justice Charles presiding. Appearing for the Crown were Mr Blair and Mr Parry, and representing Dukes were Mr Cottingham and Mr Jordan. The local newspaper, the Bury Times, reported the proceedings almost verbatim and noted that as he entered the dock it could be seen that Dukes had taken some trouble over his appearance. He was dressed in a brownish-grey overcoat with a pocket handkerchief in the breast pocket, wore a new collar and tie and had his hair neatly brushed. Thrusting his hands into his coat pockets, he kept them there until he had pleaded 'Not guilty', in a low voice, to the charge of murdering George Gordon.

Mr Blair opened the case for the prosecution, setting out the known details of the crime in chronological order. The jury were told how it was Dukes's job to buy and sell goods at the shop and so it was necessary from time to time for him to account for the proceeds. For several weeks Dukes had been using delaying tactics, including sending a letter to his employers purporting to come from C. Alstead of Lime Tree House, Prestwich, saying that he wished to buy a considerable amount of furniture. On the morning of the tragedy George Gordon arrived at the shop as arranged, but Dukes, who had been in the Lord Nelson public house just five doors away, did not appear until about a quarter to two – although he knew that Gordon was waiting to see him. Young Tootill and the carter, Fowler, were sent off to Prestwich to deliver the furniture to what turned out to be a non-existent address and by the time they returned, Dukes was in the shop on his own. Tootill gave evidence about carrying the locked wardrobe into the back warehouse and PC Bremner told the court that when Dukes was set upon by Meyer Gordon he had said, 'I have not murdered him, but I will tell you all about it.' PC McLellan and Sergeant Ross then gave evidence about the discovery of the body. The Clerk of Arraigns suddenly became agitated and had a conversation with the judge. It appeared that there were two books in the witness box, of similar size, one a bible and the other the Five Books of Moses, on which the Jewish witnesses were to swear. It appeared that there had been some confusion and that witnesses might have sworn on the wrong book. Sergeant Ross agreed that he had used the Five Books of Moses, and was required to give his evidence again after swearing on the bible. Shortly afterwards, the court adjourned for the day.

The next morning the first witness was Dr Robert Mitchell, who told the court that he had examined George Gordon's body and had found an incision 1¼in in length on the back of the head and another slightly smaller at the top of the right ear, the skull being fractured. There were five wounds to the forehead and further skull fractures, the right cheekbone being completely smashed and the upper jawbone also fractured. Death would have been caused either by the injury at the back of the skull or that on the frontal bone. He had examined the fire grate at the house and had found blood spots and brain on the fender, more bloodstains on the floor near the door to a length of 38in, and the trousers worn by the accused had blood spots on both legs. Cross-examined by Mr Cunningham, Dr Mitchell said that he did not think that Gordon's falling back and hitting his head on the fender could have caused any of the skull fractures.

This evidence concluded the case for the prosecution, but before the defence could call any witnesses the court heard that the accused man wished to make a statement. The judge agreed that he could do this and Dukes stood up in the dock, grasping the rails, and began to speak quietly but firmly. He told the court that he had deliberately absented himself from work on the morning of the murder as he had been drinking and he did not wish Mr Gordon to know this. When he did arrive at the shop, he could see that Gordon was annoyed, complaining that he had five weeks' accounts to look through and, as it was the Jewish New Year that evening, he had decided to take the books back to Manchester. Picking up the ledgers, he made as if to leave and then decided that he would first look at the furniture that Dukes had told him was due to go to Prestwich. One of the items was a large mirror in a gilt frame that was hanging on the wall and Gordon helped Dukes to get it down. Dukes took the mirror into the back warehouse where, in placing it on the table, he let it slip and the mirror came out of the frame, although it did not break. Gordon was incensed and threatened to sack Dukes on the spot. Dukes coolly replied that he could do what he liked but he must not strike him, at which Gordon shouted, 'Who the devil do you

Below and opposite: Death certificate of William Dukes, showing Christmas Eve as date of execution. (© Crown Copyright)

think you are talking to?' and rushed at him, waving the hammer. Dukes managed to evade the first rush, but Gordon came at him again and in the ensuing struggle fell back on the fender in the fireplace, hitting it with the back of his head. Pleading that his mind was still fuddled with the amount of drink he had taken, Dukes said that he might have struck Gordon on the forehead with the hammer, but it was in self-defence. He believed that Gordon would have killed him if he had not defended himself; at that, he appeared to have run out of words and sat down.

Mr Blair, summing up for the prosecution, said that the accused's statement had put a different complexion on things. Now Dukes was trying to get the charge reduced to one of manslaughter, a conclusion that Blair thought the jury could not come to. It was clear that the Gordons were suspicious of Dukes and that Gordon had returned home to discuss the matter with his father before confronting Dukes later in the day. The fact that Dukes had been in drink was no reason for him to avoid his employer, and there was not one particle of evidence that could lead to a reduction in the charge to manslaughter. Young Tootill and the carter Fowler had both seen Dukes during a large part of the day, but neither of them had been called by the defence to answer questions on the subject of how affected by drink he had been. No witness had been called in support of Dukes's story about the mirror being damaged and George Gordon's reaction to that; neither was there any evidence to connect George Gordon with the hammer. Blair concluded by telling the jury that if they found that there was any evidence of blows struck by Gordon, they must give the accused the full benefit of it.

Mr Cottingham, for the defence, agreed that the jury must have been shocked at the details of the discovery of George Gordon's body and that it must certainly have influenced them and may have clouded their minds, so possibly preventing them from arriving at a right verdict. It was not in Dukes's interest to kill his employer, for if the employer went, so did Dukes's living. He had told lies, but that did not necessarily make him a murderer and he certainly appeared to have been making every effort to avoid Gordon on the day of the murder, rather than confronting him. The

Fracture and dislocation & nearly hanging pursuant to sentence of Law	Certificate received from Fred Price Coroner for the County of Lancashire Inquest held Twenty fourth December 1889	Twenty Seventh December 1889	Omas Holbrook Registrar

THE BURY MURDER.—EXECUTION OF DUKES.

William Dukes was executed in Strangeways Gaol, Manchester, on Tuesday morning, for the murder of Wm. Gordon, at Bury, on September 25th. From the time of his conviction till Monday, Dukes, though not indifferent to his fate, contemplated his impending doom with equanimity. On Monday, however, there was a marked change in his demeanour. He was obviously depressed, and during the night he slept little, being very restless. On Tuesday morning he woke early, and wanted to get up, but was tranquillised. He ate a fairly good breakfast, and as the hour fixed for the execution approached he did not flinch. He looked pale when just after eight o'clock had struck he appeared on the scaffold. He had previously asked Berry, the executioner, whether he would be permitted to say anything, and seeing the reporters in the prison yard below the scaffold, which projects from a corridor leading from the condemned cell, he said, "Tell my wife that I die happy." It was raining heavily at the time, and when the bolt was drawn water splashed from the platform into the well beneath. The culprit died without a tremor, and there was a marked absence of muscular twitching after death. Being a man under 10st. weight, he was given a drop of 6ft.

THE CRIME.

Mr. Justice Charles, before whom Dukes was tried at the last Manchester Assizes, intimated that in his opinion the verdict of the jury finding the man guilty of wilful murder was the only just conclusion at which they could have arrived. The fact that since the man's condemnation there had been no general effort to obtain a reprieve shows how universally the public concurred with the judgment. In many respects the case was an exceedingly painful one. George Gordon, the victim of the tragedy, was a young man of Jewish descent. He was in partnership with his father and brother, carrying on business as the Gordon Furnishing Company, at Manchester, with branches in Bury, Burnley, and other towns. William Dukes, a young married man, respectably connected, had the management of the Bury shop. For some time he discharged his duties satisfactorily, but eventually he got drinking and acquired other loose habits, which led to the business being neglected. On Wednesday, Sept. 25, George Gordon was sent over from Manchester to Bury to make some investigations. He was seen at the Bury shop during the day by several persons employed there. These people were sent away by Dukes on one pretext or another, and thus George Gordon and Dukes were left in the place together. The former was never seen alive afterwards. That same night Dukes despatched a telegram to Manchester in Gordon's name, purporting to inform the young man's father that he had gone to Burnley, and would return on the following day. When, however, George did not make his appearance at home in due course inquiries were instituted, and it was found that he had not been to the Burnley shop at all. Then his father and brother became alarmed, and, going over to Bury, they obtained the assistance of the police, and instituted a search through the premises. They found nothing for some time, though it was noticed that several flags had been loosened in the cellar. Later, however, Mr. Simeon Gordon had his attention attracted to a wardrobe which was in the storeroom at the back, and he immediately asked to have it opened. Dukes told him it was sold, and had to go to Rochdale, and when pressed to open it he said the key was not at hand. This conduct of his aroused suspicion, and the father insisted on having the wardrobe broken open. The order was obeyed, and on the doors being forced open a terrible discovery was made. Inside the wardrobe lay the body of George Gordon. It had been doubled up, so as to crowd it into the recess. The head was shockingly battered, the face bruised, the throat cut, and one of the eyes almost forced out. Round about the place were marks of blood, partially covered with whitening and varnished, but not successfully concealed. There were also discovered in the vicinity a hammer and a chisel, both of which had blood stains upon them. Dukes, on these discoveries being made, was immediately apprehended. At the outset he said to those around him, "I'll tell you all about it," but he vouchsafed no further explanation until he was on his trial at the assizes. Then, with the permission of the Judge, he made a statement to the effect that George Gordon threatened him with violence. "As deceased was running at me," he added, "I put my heels behind his and threw him, and he came down on the fender with the back of his head, and in my passion and having drink in me I really do not know what took place after. I believe I did strike him on the forehead with the hammer. It might equally have been my life that might have been taken as his if I had not defended myself." Medical and other evidence, however, did not in any way tend to confirm the assertion of Dukes that the act was committed in self-defence. On the contrary, it showed that the victim had been subjected to brutish, demoniacal violence for which there could have been no possible justification. Unquestionably, the finding of the jury was the only one that could be deemed consistent with justice. Dukes since his condemnation has taken matters very calmly, and he never seems to have anticipated for a moment that he could escape the doom which had been pronounced upon him after a protracted and most searching trial.

A contemporary account of Dukes's execution. (Accrington Observer)

fender was quite stout enough to have caused a fracture of the skull as Gordon fell against it and it had been shown that there were hairs sticking to it – unlike the hammer, upon which there were none. The truth was that Gordon had attacked Dukes, had been repulsed and thrown down on the fender and had then been attacked with the hammer while Dukes was in an entirely understandable and uncontrollable passion. If the accused had taken drink, then he would be even more likely to have lost control in those circumstances. Cottingham further challenged the prosecution to point out any evidence that went to show that the prisoner had premeditated means for the disposal of the body of the dead man. During this speech, Dukes repeatedly broke down and held his head in his hands. The judge told the jury that it was for them to decide whether the crime was one of murder or manslaughter, but that he could not see how they could find for a complete acquittal. The jury then retired, taking only thirteen minutes to bring in a verdict of 'Guilty of wilful murder'. The judge, donning the black cap, told Dukes that the jury could not have arrived at any other verdict and sentenced him to death.

The Home Secretary having refused to commute the sentence to life imprisonment, William Dukes was hanged at Strangeways on, of all days, Christmas Eve 1889 by James Berry, a former policeman turned hangman. Berry was one of a new breed of executioner who studied his craft, made sure that the execution was over in the shortest possible time so as to reduce the suffering of the condemned person and strove to produce instant death, rather than death by strangulation. In this he was successful, although he later turned to drink, resigning his position as executioner in 1891 and becoming an evangelist.

On the fatal morning Dukes awoke early, having slept little, but after being given a tranquilliser to calm him down, he ate a fairly good breakfast. Interest in the case was considerable and the Accrington Observer reported fully on the execution and the crime for which it had been ordained, noting that it was a foul morning and that outside in the prison yard the rain was bouncing off the scaffold, which stood in the open air. When Berry walked into the condemned cell Dukes asked him if he would be allowed to say something when he got to the scaffold, and the executioner told him that he would. Once pinioned and standing on the open-air drop, just before the white cap was placed over his head and Berry launched him into eternity, Dukes told the newspaper reporters gathered in the prison yard below the scaffold, 'Tell my wife that I die happy.'

3

TRIPLE MURDER

Lancaster, 1905

With the exception of the old Newgate Prison in London, Lancaster Castle has seen more death sentences handed out than any other court in England. Crowds of several thousands used to flock to watch public executions outside the castle, until the Capital Punishment within Prisons Bill (1868) directed that all future executions would take place within the confines of the prison. The last execution at Lancaster took place on Tuesday 15 November 1910 (the first since 1887), when hangman John Ellis and his assistant Thomas Pierrepoint dispatched Thomas Rawcliffe for the murder of his wife Louisa Ann.

In 1911 the 'Court Keeper' of the castle was 57-year-old William Hodgson Bingham, whose job it was to act as caretaker and official guide to the Crown Court and Shire Hall, built at the end of the eighteenth century. The Crown Court had a long history of extremely harsh treatment of prisoners, many of whom were sentenced to death or transportation for what would be regarded nowadays as comparatively trivial offences. Bingham lived in lodgings inside the castle, together with his son James Henry Bingham and his daughter Edith Agnes. There was also another daughter – Nellie, aged 36 – who lived close by, and three other siblings dotted around the area. On 22 January of that year, William fell ill with sickness and diarrhoea and died the following day. In his will he left his eight-day clock and the secretaire 'left me by my mother' to his married sister Margaret Crookhall Cottam, together with two houses and a shop and premises called Duncan Cottage at Myerscough, and two fields at Bilsborough. All the rest of his estate was to be held in trust for his wife Elizabeth, who was to have a life interest, and thereafter the estate was to be divided among his six children: Margaret, James Henry, Nellie, William Edward jr, Gertrude Annie and Edith Agnes. In the event Bingham's wife had predeceased him, so the six children shared the residual estate of around £3,000 between them, and after the funeral the 37-year-old James Henry was appointed Court Keeper in place of his father.

John O'Gaunt Gateway, entrance to Lancaster Castle, c. 1904. (Author's collection)

A certain amount of friction grew up between James and his sister Edith Agnes, who was now keeping house for him. The late William Bingham had often complained that Edith was too flighty; that she did not give sufficient consideration to her housekeeping duties, told untruths and had a propensity to get into debt – and now James was starting to be of the same opinion. He arranged for his sister Margaret (Maggie), who was working in the Prison Service at Hull Prison, to take some leave and keep house for him; she arrived on 18 July. Maggie was on good terms with Edith Agnes, but had received instructions from James that she must keep a careful eye on the girl, although Edith appeared to show no signs of resentment at the presence of her sister. On the day following her arrival Maggie became ill with sickness and diarrhoea and died, rather unexpectedly, on 23 July. She was buried with her father at Lancaster Cemetery.

Edith and Nellie stayed on at the castle to look after their brother, although Nellie later left and moved to Manchester. Another sister, Gertrude Annie, called to see her brother on Friday 11 August and a discussion took place about Edith Agnes, who was still giving him cause for concern. The two searched Edith's clothes while she was out, as James was suspicious that Edith was getting into debt once more, but they found nothing. James grumbled that Edith was again failing in her household duties, was not keeping the cooking utensils clean and was not cooking his meals properly, so he proposed to take on a housekeeper, Mrs Mary Cox-Walker. She had been a nurse at the Lancaster County Asylum and, although not a relative, had known the family for the past twenty-five years.

The cleaning lady, Annie Sampson, came as usual on 11 August and worked with Edith cleaning the rooms and preparing for the arrival of the new housekeeper, whom Edith told her had been summoned by her brother. While they worked James came into the kitchen and Edith said to him, 'We want something for our dinner, Jimmie.' James made no reply, but a short time later Annie Sampson noticed a plate with a large piece of meat on it, which Edith placed in a frying pan and cooked. Later on Edith said to the cleaner, 'There is not much left. I think he has eaten it all.'

On Saturday 12 August Dr James Wilson Macintosh, of Mayo House, Lancaster, received a call from the castle and found James in bed suffering from a vomiting fit. The steak that he had eaten for supper the previous evening appeared to have disagreed with him and he had cramps in his ankles, from which he could get no relief despite constant massaging of his lower limbs. Perhaps remembering the recent death of William Bingham, Dr Macintosh became suspicious and gave orders that all the vomit must be retained; when he called again on Sunday there were seven or eight pints waiting for him. Macintosh took the liquid away and made tests that convinced him there was arsenic present in considerable quantities. He therefore arranged for Mary Cox-Walker to come in straight away to care for the sick man.

Her statement to the police, included in the trial papers, indicated that Dr Macintosh told her, 'You are to keep a watch on everything and you are to make certain that no one gives any food to Mr Bingham except yourself. Please make certain that you take in the milk from the doorstep and that no one else meddles with it.' Although he did not specifically mention poison, the doctor cautioned Mrs Cox-Walker, 'Be very careful about your own food', leaving her to work out the reason for this for herself.

On the morning of 14 August James seemed a little better. He had been sick only once in the night and had been able to take a little bread and milk, so Dr Macintosh decided that he would not need to call again until 8 p.m. By the time he did so James had had a relapse, with much vomiting and again complaining of cramp. The doctor decided that he should be moved immediately to the nearby house of Matthew Henry Cottam (whose wife was the late William Bingham's sister and the major beneficiary of his will), where he could be better looked after. Mrs Cox-Walker agreed to share the nursing duties. On Tuesday 15 August at 1.15 a.m. she handed over her patient to Mrs Cottam, but by the time she came back on duty at about 5.30 a.m. James was dead. Apart from Mr and Mrs Cottam, present at the death were William Edward Bingham jr and Edith Agnes.

A post-mortem was performed by Dr William Henry Roberts MSc, Fellow of the Institute of Chemistry of Great Britain and chief assistant to the County Analyst; his report (now held at the National Archives) shows that one end of the stomach was very inflamed and one patch was a very dark red. The stomach contained about $\frac{1}{400}$ of a grain of white arsenic and the kidneys $\frac{1}{65}$ of a grain. The liver tested weighed about 9$\frac{1}{5}$ ounces and contained around $\frac{1}{12}$ grain; as the average human adult liver weighs around 3$\frac{1}{2}$lb, that meant the whole liver would have contained around half a grain. The spleen also contained white arsenic, as did the contents of the stomach, and Dr Roberts formed the opinion that there must have been more than a poisonous dose of arsenic in the body and that James Bingham had died from acute arsenical poisoning. An inquest was opened and adjourned until 14 September and an immediate search of the castle was ordered, carried out by Sergeant Johnson accompanied by Gertrude Bingham. Buried under some old rush chairs in a little-used corner of the courtroom they found a large watering can, which Gertrude said had been used for spreading weedkiller on the outside Parade. There were also some empty tins of 'Acme' weedkiller, marked 'Poison'.

Nellie Bingham, now living at Barton-on-Irwell, received a letter from her sister Edith, dated 14 August, which she handed to the police, telling them that her sister was 'queer at times and difficult to manage'. The letter read as follows:

Dear Nellie,
I am just writing you a few lines to ask you if you will come over and get me away from here as I can not stand it any longer. They are making it harder every day for me. Mrs Cottam has come on Sunday night and her girls are buying in for her. I think that things are coming to a past [sic] now. Our Willie and his girl are never away, you know what she is doing it for. Aunts M & A are up in a morning till last thing at night, jumping on me all the time so you will see what times I am having. I never had anything to eat in the house all last week. When I get away, you can write a letter to them and say you will not let me stay with them. Mrs C. says I will have to do all. Do not forget to come soon for me, if not I will do something at myself because I cannot stand it. I have not seen Charlie, the boy I go with, everybody seems to be my enemy. Do not let them know I have written to you. They are all in the front place while I is in the back place. They say I can go but you come on tomorrow and write as soon as you get this letter and let me know what train you will

come on so I can get down to meet you. Dear Nellie, I must ask you to come soon. Do you think Mrs Casson will have me for a bit? I went up to mother's grave on Sunday night with flowers. They are all saying such cutting things to me so you will see it is making me quite ill. I must ask you not to forget to come for me. I will not leave Lancaster as C is in Lancaster for a while. Mr Timmins [one of the Court guides] says I should get away some as it is making him ill too. He told our William he had said other to me. I hope you are well over there, with love, Edith.
P.S. Do come Tuesday at the castle. I will pay you back in the end.*

On the late afternoon of Wednesday 30 August Inspector John Whitfield and Detective Sergeant Johnson visited Edith, who was now staying with the Cottams, and Whitfield told her, 'I am going to arrest you on a serious charge of wilfully administering poison to your brother James and causing his death.' Edith was taken down to the police station, where she made a statement as follows:

I never did anything of the sort. I had someone in the house when I prepared dinner and the meat was bought by Jimmy alone. I don't know how you can accuse me of it, Mr Whitfield. I done nothing. Mrs Sampson was there when I cooked the steak. I did not see my brother again until 3 o'clock and he told me he felt sick and he sent me out for a bottle of soda water, which I got in a siphon at Bensons. That weedkiller was used by my father and Jimmy last year and we used to fill it in the witness room.

At this point Inspector Whitfield leant forward and said to Edith, 'Bear in mind that I have not mentioned weedkiller to you.' Edith replied, 'I mentioned the weedkiller as I thought of mentioning it at the Town Hall when they were talking about it at the inquest.' At that juncture, Edith was charged and eventually committed for trial at the next Lancashire Assizes on 26 October. In the meantime the bodies of William Hodgson Bingham and Margaret Bingham were exhumed; both were found to contain more than a fatal dose of arsenic.

The trial began on 28 October in front of Mr Justice Avory, a man known for his calm, unemotional temperament and considered in his latter years to be a 'legal encyclopedia'. This was one of his first great murder cases and the trial attracted a considerable amount of attention. Mr Langdon KC and Mr Gordon Hewart (later to become Lord Chief Justice) appeared for the

---

* The original letter, a transcript of which is now at the National Archives, was full of spelling mistakes and other errors, some of which have been corrected here for clarity.

Crown and a member of a prominent local family, Mr Wingate-Saul, led for the defence. Edith was now charged not only with the murder of her brother but also of her father and her sister, whose original death certificates had certified death by 'gastric catarrh/heart failure' and 'brain tumour' respectively, but had now been changed to 'death by arsenical poisoning'. The prosecution led with the results of the post-mortems and the fact that Edith was known to have quarrelled with her brother James. Mrs Sampson told the court that she had seen James's sister cook the steak but that, although Edith did eat meat on occasion, she had not done so on that particular day.

The next witness was Charles Emerson, a cinematograph operator living in Preston, the man to whom Edith had referred as her boyfriend when writing to Nellie. His statement, held at the National Archives, reveals that he had known Edith only since the previous June, and after that he had seen her several times in Lancaster and Kendal. When he first met her she was in mourning for her father and claimed that she had inherited wealth on his

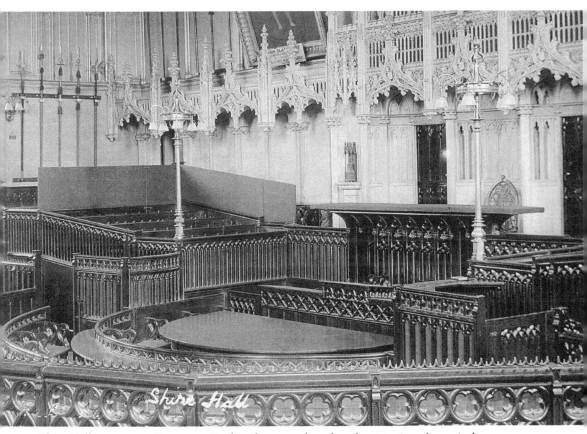

Shire Hall courtroom, Lancaster Castle, where searchers found empty tins of arsenical weedkiller. It was the scene of the trial of Edith Bingham. (Author's collection)

demise. She told him that she had fallen out with her brother because of his intemperance; Emerson said that sometimes she would be very bitter towards James, but at other times she could be completely the opposite. The couple had exchanged presents but, although it had been spoken about, they were not engaged. Nellie then took the stand and was questioned about the letter that her sister had written to her asking to be taken away from the castle, but had little further to add.

The next witness was Francis Massey, a drysalter, who told the court that he had supplied the Binghams with 'Acme' weedkiller on several occasions, including two gallons to William Bingham in July and August 1909, plus a further gallon in June 1910; and that he had also supplied James Bingham with two gallons in May 1911. Dr Roberts acknowledged receiving a separate tin of the weedkiller as a control and said that it had contained one gallon of a pale, straw-coloured liquid which on analysis turned out to be a strong solution of arsenic in alkali. The arsenic content was a little over 2lb to the gallon and so ten drops of this liquid would have contained two grains of white arsenic, which is an average fatal dose – the weedkiller was obviously dangerous stuff. 'Ten drops in half a tumbler of water would taste like a dilute solution of carbonate of soda,' said Dr Roberts, and he also confirmed that more than a fatal dose could be put on a steak and would not taste when the meat was cooked. At this stage things were looking black for Edith, who promptly collapsed and had to be led from court, coming back an hour later apparently fully recovered.

Counsel for the prosecution then summed up, basing his case on the known presence of arsenic in the castle and the fact that arsenic could not have got into the steak by accident. There were also the major facts that no fewer than three residents of the castle had died within months of each other, and that Edith had been living in the castle at all material times.

The defence produced no witnesses and Wingate-Saul said, quite correctly, that it was no job of his to prove how the deceased persons had taken arsenic. He added that Edith had no motive for committing the crimes, as she would lose by the death of her relatives and would also be cast out into the street once James died. Both James and Margaret had died intestate and Edith would receive no benefit from their deaths.*

Mr Justice Avory then addressed the jury and started his remarks by saying that, 'In cases of poisoning the law implies malice. If it is proved that any person administered poison to another or laid poison for him, there is no

---

* This was probably not true, as any estate they left would have been divided among their next of kin, unless Edith was found guilty of their murder, in which case Edith's share would go to her siblings.

need for the prosecution to show a motive,' and went on, 'I must ask you to decide whether the prisoner's brother, James Bingham, died from arsenical poisoning and if so, whether the prisoner wilfully administered the poison to him. On the first point,' he continued, 'there can be no doubt, if the medical evidence is to be believed; but there is no evidence that the arsenic was in the steak and James Bingham could have ingested the poison at any time during the day. In regard to Margaret Bingham's death it is not easy to see how, if the prisoner introduced arsenic into the food of the breakfast in July, she managed to ensure that Margaret, and no one else, should eat the poisoned food. There is no evidence that the father took food cooked by the prisoner just before he was taken ill and the weedkiller tins found at the castle were empty. Surely if the accused had been using the weedkiller to poison her family, she would have taken care to get rid of the tins instead of allowing them to remain in the castle for anyone to find them?' The judge then disposed of any reference to Edith being 'queer' by telling the jury, 'There is no evidence that the prisoner is not responsible in law for her action.'

Avory's parting shot to the jury was, 'The jury must consider the behaviour of the prisoner when the deaths took place. All the evidence suggests that she was distressed in all three cases and if the evidence amounts only to this, that the accused had an opportunity of administering the poison but that it was possible the poison had been accidentally introduced into the food taken by James, then you must acquit her.'

Expecting the jury to be out for a long time, many of the people in the public gallery had brought lunch, thinking that they would be able to eat their meal in the comfort of the courtroom. Unfortunately for them everyone was peremptorily ordered outside, so they settled for a picnic within the castle grounds instead. When word came that the jury were coming back there was an almighty rush for the doors and the courtroom was so packed that, on his way back into court, Mr Justice Avory had to step over the prostrate body of a woman who had fainted just outside the judge's door. The jury had taken just twenty minutes to find Edith Bingham not guilty on the charge of murdering James Bingham and the prosecution then told the court that no evidence would be offered in the cases of William and Margaret Bingham. Edith was formally found 'Not Guilty' and discharged.

This news was received with cheers in the courtroom, although here and there could be heard a few hisses, which the judge silenced immediately. It was generally believed in the town that Edith Bingham was lucky and that, owing to lack of evidence, she had escaped the gallows by the skin of her teeth. 'Who else had the motive and opportunity,' people wondered, 'and who else was resident in the castle on the occasion of all three deaths?' After she was freed Edith sank into obscurity and now, more than ninety years on, we are never likely to know for certain whether she was guilty or innocent.

4

THE BRIDES
IN THE BATH

Blackpool, 1913

Blackpool has been one of the prime holiday resorts of the British Isles for well over 100 years and its Tower still stands as proudly today as it did when it was built in 1894, a replica of the Eiffel Tower in Paris. Due east of the Tower and about half a mile away from it is Regent Road, in 1913, as now, consisting mainly of hotels and boarding houses built to cater for the masses who pour into the town during the holiday season each year. Nowadays greatly improved to meet the demands of the modern holidaymaker, the houses in Regent Road at the time of the First World War had only partial gas or electric lighting, which meant that – along with the chamber pot (for there were few houses with indoor 'facilities' in those days) – the guest would be given a candle to light his way to bed.

On the early evening of 10 December 1913 the casual observer might have noticed a couple walking from the North Station along Talbot Road onto the Promenade, where they stood looking at the Tower in amazement. The man was about 40 years of age, of slender build, with dark hair turning grey; he was clean shaven, had a pock-marked face with a large mouth and long thin nose, and he walked with his feet turned out. The woman clutched her male companion's arm tightly as they took in the scene, as well she might, since she had married him only five weeks before and 25-year-old Alice Smith, née Burnham, gurgled with delight as her new husband promised to take her on the Giant Wheel which stood a little further along the promenade. George Joseph Smith, a man who claimed to be of 'independent means', already knew that the wheel was closed for the winter and that his money was safe.

Alice was barely 5ft tall, rather heavily built, and until recently had been working as a nurse in Southsea. She had long been conscious that there were few jobs for single women of the lower middle classes at the start of the twentieth century, apart from the roles of lady's maid or governess – both of which had little social standing and even less pay – or nursing. It was vital,

Blackpool Tower and wheel, c. 1914. (Author's collection)

therefore, that a young woman should find herself a decent husband at the earliest opportunity, to avoid being left firmly 'on the shelf'. Alice attended the local Methodist chapel in Southsea and, one Sunday in the autumn of 1913, she had made the acquaintance of the man to whom she was now married. He had been smartly dressed, with starched wing collar and a tightly knotted tie, polite and attentive: somehow he always managed to be in the next pew at Sunday service. Before long, to her delight and heartfelt relief, she was able to announce to her friends that she and George were 'walking out'. Her fiancé seemed very interested in money and took great care to show her his bankbook, at the same time making a casual enquiry as to Alice's means. She was delighted to tell him that her family lived at Aston Clinton, Buckinghamshire, where her father was a fruit grower and, in an era when young single women were generally regarded as being 'unsafe' with money, Mr Burnham was holding about £100 in cash for her, in addition to which she had nearly £30 in the Post Office. She had also loaned her sister the sum

George Joseph Smith.
(Stewart Evans)

of £10, which was still outstanding. In the context of the times Alice was 'comfortable', both physically and financially.

In a remarkably short time George Smith had proposed marriage and although Alice thought, at first, that the difference in their ages could be a drawback, a girl did not receive a proposal of marriage every day of the week and finally to come off 'the shelf' would be a great comfort. Besides, her fiancé appeared to be a man of some means and was offering her a comfortable future and freedom from the loneliness of a life in a succession of single rooms in cheap, seaside boarding houses. On 15 October 1913 Alice wrote to her parents, giving them her good news that she was now engaged to be married and telling them that her fiancé, being an honourable man, considered that he should meet his future in-laws without delay. The Burnhams, somewhat surprised by this turn of events but not wishing to appear unwelcoming, responded by inviting the couple to spend a few days with them. George wrote back to say that they would arrive at around 4 o'clock on the afternoon of 25 October.

When they arrived home Alice, looking nervous and rather flushed, introduced George to her parents and for the first few hours everything seemed to be going well. George told Mr and Mrs Burnham a little about himself: he said that he was a man of independent means, the son of George Thomas Smith (an artist and painter of flowers), and he explained that he and Alice had loved each other on sight and were now wishing to get married at the earliest possible date. Despite these protestations of good faith, Mr and Mrs Burnham began to have their doubts about their future son-in-law whose manner, once his guard dropped, seemed a little coarse for their middle-class tastes and who was not the sort of man they had dreamed about for their darling Alice. Mr Burnham confronted his daughter and suggested that she was perhaps being somewhat hasty and that an engagement of several months

Alice Burnham, Smith's second 'bride in the bath'. (Stewart Evans)

might be advisable, so that the couple could get to know one another rather better. To his sorrow, Alice rejected this suggestion out of hand and words became heated, during which Mr Burnham reluctantly, but still thinking of his daughter, ordered Smith out of the house. Smith left, taking Alice with him.

Ten days later the couple were married at Portsmouth Register Office and the newly-weds took furnished rooms at 80 Kimberley Road, Southsea, until they could look round for something more permanent. 'Now we are married, my dear,' said George to his new wife, 'we must have a little talk about money.' Alice looked doubtful, but was reassured when her husband proposed that they should each make a will, leaving everything to each other, and also that they should insure Alice's life for the sum of £500, the £25 premium for which could come out of her bank savings. In addition, George gently suggested that perhaps the £100 which her father was holding for her would be better in her hands than her father's; Alice promptly wrote a letter, asking that the funds be sent immediately. Her father wrote back saying that as Alice's husband was of independent means, he would like to hang on to the money for the time being, a letter which turned George Smith to rage. He wrote a high-handed and insulting reply to Mr Burnham, asking, 'What earthly right have you to scorn your daughter so? Is the record of your family so full of virtue that you describe and begrudge your daughter's bright prospects? Regarding the matter that the £100 and interest should stand over – a more foolish and illegal action I have never heard. The money is payable on demand, failing which I will take the matter up myself without further delay.' Mr Burnham no doubt thought that such a rude and uncalled-for missive did not deserve the favour of a reply and another letter from Smith soon followed the first, this time demanding on behalf of his wife that the money should be forwarded to her forthwith, failing which 'I shall be compelled to take the usual course in order to secure the sum referred to.' Alice followed this up with a letter of her own, rather more equable in tone but insisting, all the same, that her money should be forthcoming, otherwise she would have no option but to seek the help of the law.

The Burnhams were now growing increasingly worried about their daughter and the man she had married within less than three months of meeting him, and they sought the advice of a solicitor, who wrote to Southsea making further enquiries. Almost gibbering with rage, Smith penned a postcard to Mr Burnham which said, 'Sir, In answer to your application regarding my parentage etc., my mother was a Buss Horse, my father a Cab Driver, my sister a rough rider over the arctic regions – my brothers were all gallant sailors on a steam-roller. This is the only information I can give to those who are not entitled to ask such questions. Your despised Son-in-Law, G. Smith.' Further postcards followed and finally, having consulted his solicitor yet again, Burnham was advised that he had no option but to accede to his daughter's request and so a cheque for £104 1s 1d was dispatched post haste, receipt of which Alice acknowledged on 1 December. Shortly afterwards her sister received a request for repayment of the £10 loan, which she refunded without comment. Alice was now well and truly at loggerheads with her family.

Now, after having made the long and tiring rail journey from Portsmouth to Blackpool, the couple walked past the Tower and turned left into Adelaide Street. As it was out of season, many of the boarding houses displayed 'No vacancy' signs, but they knocked at the door of no. 65, which was opened by the proprietor, Mrs Susanna Marsden. She told the couple that she did have a bedroom available and took them upstairs to see it. 'That is acceptable,' said the man, 'but do you have a bath?' 'I'm afraid not', was the reply. 'In that case, the room will not do.' 'I'm sorry about that,' the landlady said, sensing her customers slipping away but at the same time wishing to make the best of a bad job. 'If you walk to the end, turn right at Regent Road and go to number 16, the lady there might well be able to help you.'

The boarding house at no. 16 was rented by a widow, Mrs Margaret Crossley, who ran it with the assistance of her daughter-in-law Alice and her son

Regent Road, Blackpool, where George Joseph Smith killed Alice Burnham, his second 'bride in the bath'. They lodged at no. 16. (Author)

Joseph. Not only did she have a room – in fact, until the Smiths arrived, the boarding house was completely empty of guests – but there was also a bath, a piece of information which seemed to please the prospective guests as they were shown into a first-floor bed-sitting room overlooking the street. The bathroom was along a short corridor and situated over the downstairs kitchen, the bath itself being cased in brown wood and positioned against one wall. Smith paid Mrs Crossley the 10s that she asked as deposit and then he and Alice went to collect their baggage from the station, before enjoying the tea prepared by their landlady. Later they went out again, turning right out of the boarding house and left into Church Street where, at no. 121, Dr George Billing had his surgery. George Smith explained to the doctor that his wife was suffering from recurrent headaches and, noting that Alice was somewhat overweight, Dr Billing decided that she was suffering from no more than constipation and prescribed accordingly.

The following day, Thursday 11 December, Mrs Crossley discussed with Smith the arrangements for meals and they decided that if the Smiths provided meat and other items, Mrs Crossley would cook them. After lunch Alice complained of a slight headache – 'Something', she said, 'probably brought on by the long journey the day before', although she told Mrs Crossley that she had enjoyed a good night's sleep. That evening the landlady noticed Alice writing a postcard, which her husband appeared to be dictating. It was addressed to Alice's mother and said: 'My Dear Mother, We arrived here on Wednesday. I have again suffered from bad headaches. My husband does all that he possibly can. Alice.'

The next day Alice requested a hot bath in the evening; Alice Crossley confirmed that the bathroom had hot and cold running water with a gas lamp to provide illumination and promised to have the bath ready at around 8 o'clock. The Smiths returned at that time and went upstairs just as the Crossleys were sitting down to their evening meal in the back kitchen. A few minutes later, Mrs Crossley looked up from her plate and drew the attention of her son and daughter-in-law to a rivulet of water that had dampened the ceiling and was now running down the wall. 'Alice,' said Mrs Crossley, 'you had better go up and tell them about having too much water in the bath.' 'Oh,' replied Alice, 'we can't do that; these people will think that they're not welcome. Let's leave it and see if it happens again.'

Just then Smith came in, seemingly oblivious to the water running down the wall, and handed the landlady a couple of eggs for their breakfast. As he left the room he called upstairs, 'Alice, do remember to put the light out when you have finished.' Alice Crossley misheard and went out to see what the lodger wanted. 'No,' he said, 'I was calling to my wife and she does not answer me.' Smith went up the stairs and into the bathroom, but came out immediately shouting, 'My wife cannot speak to me. Get Dr Billing; she knows him.' The doctor arrived within minutes, to find Alice in the bath with her head being supported above the water by her husband, who had rolled up the left sleeve of his jacket. 'Whatever is the matter,' asked the doctor. 'Oh, she is drowned, she is dead', was the reply. Soapy water came to within an inch of the top of the bath and was still hot to the touch. 'Why have you not lifted your wife out of the water?' asked Billing. Smith replied that she was too heavy. 'Why then did you not pull out the plug?' 'It didn't occur to me,' said Smith. The two men struggled to lift Alice out of the bath and laid her on the bathroom floor, where a short examination by the doctor confirmed that she was dead. There being nothing more that Billing could do, he went back to his surgery, leaving Smith alone with his wife's body. Soon Smith was down in the kitchen, where Mrs Crossley told him rather brusquely that she would not allow him to sleep in the house that night. 'Why?' he said. 'I could sleep where she was.' 'I take good care that you do not,' said the woman – to which Smith replied, 'When they're dead, they're dead.' Arrangements were made for Smith to sleep in a neighbouring house that night, and he filled in the time by writing a postcard to Mrs Burnham which said, 'Dear Mother-in-Law, Alice is very ill. I will wire you tomorrow. Yours, George.' When the promised telegram eventually arrived, it said merely: 'Alice died last night in her bath. Letter follows.'

Sergeant Robert Valiant of the Blackpool Borough police called at the house and accompanied Smith back to the police station, where he made a statement setting out the details of the events of the previous two days. Valiant watched Smith closely as he made his statement and was not impressed. The widower appeared unaffected by the tragic loss of his wife, and in reply to the sergeant's question, Smith announced that he would be burying his wife at Blackpool, as 'My means are limited.'

The inquest was held on 13 December at 6.30 p.m., and by 7 it was all over. Smith described to the coroner his visit to Blackpool, his wife's feeling ill, the consultation with Dr Billing, the bath and her subsequent death. The verdict was, 'The deceased, Alice Smith came to her death at Blackpool on the 12 December 1913. The deceased suffered from heart disease and was found drowned in a hot bath, probably through being seized with a fit or faint. The cause of death was accidental.'

That same evening, Smith wrote the promised letter to his in-laws, which said:

After arriving here, Alice complained of pains in the head and went to a doctor, who examined her and gave her treatment. Yesterday, she again complained to me and the landlady of pains in the head, when she sent you and her sister a post card, after which I took her for a walk, and she appeared better later on. I found she had made arrangements with the landlady for a bath. About twenty minutes after she had entered the bath, I called out to her and got no answer and after acquainting the people in the house that something is wrong, and getting no answer, I entered the bathroom and found poor Alice with her head and shoulders under the water. The doctor who had previously attended her was sent for at my request to come, which he did. I held her head out of the water and let the water run away from her. When the doctor came, we lifted her out of the bath; he examined her and said, 'She is dead.' I then went to the police station and asked them to send an official to come to the house and take particulars, which they did. This is the greatest and most cruel shock that ever a man could have suffered. Words cannot describe my feelings. We were so happy together, which she has told all her friends in her letters to them. The people here have been very kind right through the whole time. The inquest will be held early next week [a lie – the inquest was held that very day]. I will then write to you sending all further particulars. Can you tell me her age when she had rheumatic fever and her age when she was in the Great Ormond Street Hospital?*

Smith's next action was to arrange the funeral; he met the undertaker, Mr John Hargreaves, at Regent Road to discuss the arrangements. To the undertaker's surprise Smith asked for the cheapest funeral available, suggesting that a public (or pauper's) grave would be sufficient. The following day, a Sunday, the two had another conversation, when Smith pressed for the earliest possible time for the funeral to take place. Hargreaves agreed that 12.30 p.m. on the following day was possible. Smith appeared to have given little or no thought to the Burnham family, who of course had been devastated by his news; he misled them about the inquest and did not even trouble to advise them of the time of the funeral. He must have had the shock of his life when Mrs Burnham and her son arrived at Regent Road late on Sunday morning. Now he had no choice but to give them full details of the interment, keeping to himself the fact that Alice was to go into a pauper's grave, with no headstone to mark the place. It was obvious, even to Smith, that if the Burnhams discovered what was going on there would be ructions; so after pretending to commiserate with the new arrivals, he went out to find the undertaker, asking if it was possible for his late wife to be buried in a more respectable grave of her own. 'Not possible if you want the funeral tomorrow,' Hargreaves told him. 'That would take an extra day to arrange.' 'Leave things as they are,' Smith told him. 'Put her in that public grave, but don't tell the mother.'

---

* Here Smith was either fishing, or attempting to persuade Alice's parents that her untimely death had had something to do with her previous medical history.

At noon on the following day the small group of mourners made their way to the Blackpool cemetery, where Alice Smith's coffin was lowered into a pauper's grave and Smith hastily shepherded the weeping Mrs Burnham and her son away before too many questions could be asked. It turned out that Mr Burnham had been so upset by the tragic news that he had collapsed and had not been able to travel to the funeral; so his wife and son, seeing little point in remaining in Blackpool, hurried off back to Aston Clinton to comfort him. Smith paid the funeral bill of £6 3s 9d, returned to Regent Road to collect his things and, having packed his bag, left a forwarding address written on a postcard, on the back of which Mrs Crossley later wrote, 'Wife died in bath. We shall see him again.' Hurrying away to the railway station, Smith left Mrs Crossley to ponder on the events of the past few days. It had been a great shock to have a death in the house and with the financial instincts of a seaside landlady, she blessed her lucky stars that the tragedy had not taken place in the season. Even so, she had no doubt that when the holidaymakers arrived next year they would be told soon enough by her rival landladies in Regent Road. She would have been even more upset if she had known the real situation. George Joseph Smith had been married before – in fact more than once – and his first and only real wife was still alive and living in Canada. At least one other young woman who had fallen for his wiles had drowned in her bath, and there would be a further death before Smith himself faced his maker on the gallows.

George Joseph Smith, alias George Oliver Love, alias Henry John Williams, was born in 1872 at 92 Roman Road, Bethnal Green. His father was George Thomas Smith, insurance agent, an inoffensive man who grew increasingly troubled as he failed to control his young and wayward son. At the age of 9, young George was sent to a reformatory at Gravesend for stealing and was released at the age of 16, by then thoroughly versed in the ways of the criminal. In 1891 he did six months in jail for theft, and in 1896 he went down for twelve months, in the name of George Baker, for larceny and receiving – skills no doubt first learned at the reformatory. At the age of 21 Smith had already discovered that he was attractive to a certain class of girl, usually the servant type, fearful of being left 'on the shelf' and not too bothered about her young man so long as he put a gold ring on her finger. In January 1898, at Leicester, in the name of George Oliver Love, he had married 18-year-old Caroline Beatrice Thornhill, who was given away by her brother because her father – not liking the look of her young man – had refused to attend the wedding. At that time Smith/Love was running a small bread shop which, like most of his ventures, did not prosper and he persuaded Caroline to take a series of jobs as housemaid in good-quality houses, forging references for the purpose. He then sold small items of bric-a-brac and jewellery which the unfortunate Caroline was encouraged to steal from her employers, and which in no time at all resulted in her being given a prison sentence of twelve months for stealing six silver tablespoons, four dessert forks and other items. Her husband promptly sold off all her belongings and vanished, but not before he had gone through a form of marriage with a respectable boarding-house keeper, staying with her just long enough to rob her. In November 1900 he was walking down Oxford Street in London when he was approached by a policeman and challenged, 'You are George Oliver Love.' He was protesting long and loud that his name was George Joseph Smith when his wife Caroline suddenly appeared, clutching her marriage lines to prove him a liar. He was taken away and charged with feloniously receiving stolen goods from a house in Hastings where Caroline had been employed and was given a sentence of two years for his pains. Caroline, now considerably wiser than she had been, sailed for Canada immediately.

In July 1908 Smith appeared in Bristol, where he set up as an antique and general dealer at 389 Gloucester Road. At no. 368 dwelt a young girl called Edith Mabel Pegler. She lived with her mother, who took in lodgers to keep body and soul together, and Smith was soon suggesting to Edith that she should come to work for him as his housekeeper. Within a short time she had also agreed to be his wife and over the next few years led a wandering existence, drifting from town to town, never staying in one place for long. Sometimes, her 'husband' went away on his own, leaving her to fend for herself as best she might and rarely sending her any money. Then he would suddenly reappear, often without warning, replete with cash which he claimed was the result of fortunate dealings in the antique trade. In fact he was making a living by latching on to young ladies who were more than happy to fall for his flattery and his tales of the good living they would have

For the first time the identity of 'Miss S.A.F.' is revealed. George Joseph Smith keeps to his Christian name and occupation, but this time chooses the surname 'Rose'.
Sarah Falkner (six years older than Smith) was fortunate. She lost £400 but kept her life.
(© Crown Copyright)

if only they were married. On 29 October 1909 he went through a form of marriage with Miss Sarah Annie Falkner at Southampton Register Office, under the name of George Rose, 'dealer in antiques'. Miss Falkner was aged 40 and must have been mightily relieved to have been taken 'off the shelf'; but her relief was short-lived and by November her new husband had abandoned her, taking with him all her property, amounting to some £400. The Notable British Trials book covering this case refers to the unfortunate woman only as 'Miss S.A.F.' (presumably to save her blushes) and the author believes that this is the first occasion on which her true identity has become known.

After returning to Edith, Smith soon got the wanderlust again and by midsummer 1910 he was strolling around Weymouth when he met a tall, rather shy girl called Bessie Mundy, aged 31, the possessor of a small fortune. Her father, a retired bank manager, had died leaving her £2,500 in gilt-edged securities. Her family, knowing that she was not very good with matters of finance, had persuaded her to let them put her money into a trust fund, which provided an income of around £8 a month – more than sufficient for her to live a quiet, modest existence. Although she had known Smith only a matter of hours, she consented to his proposal of marriage, the wedding certificate giving her husband's name as Henry John Williams, commercial traveller. For this special occasion he shaved off his moustache, brushed his hair and hired a morning suit and top hat, insisting that they should visit the shop of a local photographer immediately after the wedding to have their picture taken.

The first news the Mundy family had about Bessie's wedding was when a postcard arrived from her to her uncle, saying: 'Dear Uncle, I got married today. My husband is writing to you tonight. Yours truly, B. Williams.' A letter from Smith arrived shortly afterwards: 'Dear Sir, I think it is my duty to inform you of my marriage with Bessie Constance Annie Mundy at the office of the Registrar, Weymouth. Yours truly, Henry Williams.'

Once that chore had been taken care of, Smith/Williams took his new wife to the offices of local solicitor Mr W.T. Wilkinson, who at the husband's request agreed to write to the Mundy family solicitor, Mr Ponting, enquiring as to the terms of Bessie's trust fund and for a copy of the late Mr Mundy's will. Wilkinson was also asked if it was possible to obtain any of the money out of the trust fund or whether a loan could be raised on it, but he was reluctant to handle that sort of business so the couple went to another local man, Arthur Frederick Eaton, who proved more amenable. In response to Eaton's approach, Ponting sent a cheque for £135, almost all the 'free' money available, which Smith cashed immediately. That same day a telegram addressed to Henry Williams arrived at the lodgings, and while Bessie was doing some shopping Smith told the landlady that the message in the telegram meant that he would have to go away for a few days, but that he would be back soon. Later in the day a letter arrived for Bessie, the contents of which must have struck that poor lady to her very core. It read:

Dearest,
I fear you have blighted all my bright hopes of a happy future. I have caught from you a disease which is called the bad disorder. For you to be in such a state proves you could not have kept yourself morally clean . . . I don't wish to say you have had connections with another man and caught it from him, but it is either that or through not keeping yourself clean. Now for the sake of my health and honour and yours too, I must go to London and act entirely under the doctor's advice to get properly cured of this disease because it might take years before I am cured. The best thing for you to tell the landlady and everyone else is that I have gone to France. . . .'

The rest of the letter gave Bessie instructions as to what to do with the £8 per month that continued to come from her trust fund and ended, 'Mark what I say, now tear this letter up at once and throw the pieces in the road.'

Smith also addressed a letter to their landlords, Mr and Mrs Crabbe, asking that they should watch over Bessie and her finances until he came back to take control of them again. Leaving the distraught Bessie to her fate, he then returned to Edith Pegler, but in March 1912 he was off on his travels again, this time to Weston-super-Mare – another likely hunting ground for unmarried spinster ladies with money in the bank. No doubt to the surprise of both of them, Smith came across Bessie while walking on the promenade and in no time he had persuaded her to take him back, despite the misgivings of Bessie's landlady. Smith wrote a couple of unctuous letters to the Mundys offering an explanation for his actions and Bessie added a postscript to the effect that she had forgiven her husband – 'Everything after all is happening for the best and I am perfectly happy with my husband.' Smith also took the opportunity to ask for the sum of £2 10s, which was due from the trust.

Early May found the reunited couple in Herne Bay, where they took a house at a rent of £18 per annum. Mutual wills were made on 8 July, a bath was ordered from the local ironmonger the next day and on 10 July the couple visited a local surgery, where Dr French was told that Bessie had suffered from a fit the previous day. A harmless sedative was prescribed. Two days later, just after 1 a.m., Dr French was summoned to attend Bessie who, her husband said, had suffered another fit. Apart from being hot and sweaty Bessie appeared to be in good health except for a headache, for which the doctor again prescribed a sedative. The next day Bessie wrote to her uncle, telling him that she had suffered two bad fits, which had left her very weak and suffering from her nerves, but she assured him, 'My husband has been extremely kind and done all he could for me.'

The following morning Dr French received a note from Smith that said, 'Can you come at once? I am afraid my wife is dead.' Hurrying round immediately, he was taken upstairs by Smith and shown the bath in which was his wife's body, all but submerged in the water. French tried artificial respiration but without success and asked, 'How did it happen? Why did you not take her out of the water?' Smith defended himself by explaining that Bessie was too heavy for him. By midday Smith had sent a curt telegram to Mr Mundy – 'Bessie died in a fit this morning, letter following. Williams', and followed this up with an explanatory letter which carefully did not mention the possibility of an inquest being held. Bessie's brother George, however, wrote direct to the local coroner, insisting that a post-mortem should be held, followed by an inquest, and at the same time warning the coroner to 'be careful'.

The inquest, held two days later, brought in a verdict of misadventure and by the end of the year Smith, having got his hands on all of Bessie's estate, had gone back to Edith Pegler again. In September 1914 he went through a form of marriage with a servant girl, Alice Reavil, but quickly absconded back to Edith, taking with him the girl's savings of £70 and another story of a successful antique-buying campaign. Finally, in December 1914, came Smith's last escapade – the one that would prove fatal to him. On the Sunday after Christmas, 1914, the News of the World carried a paragraph headed:

FOUND DEAD IN BATH
Bride's tragic fate on Day after Wedding

Particularly sad circumstances under which a bride of a day met her death were investigated at an Islington inquest on Margaret Elizabeth Lloyd, 38, wife of a land agent of Holloway. The husband said he was married to the deceased at Bath. After travelling to London, she complained of headache and giddiness and he took her to a medical man, who prescribed for her. The following morning she said she felt much better, and during the day she went out shopping. At 7.30, she said she would have a bath and she then appeared to be cheerful. A quarter of an hour later, the witness went out and returned at a quarter past eight, expecting to see her in the sitting room. As she was not there, he enquired of the landlady and they went to the bathroom, which was in darkness. He lit the gas and then found his wife under the water, the bath being three parts full. The next day, witness found a letter among deceased's clothing, but there was nothing in it to suggest that she was likely to take her life. Dr Bates said death was due to asphyxia from drowning. The enquiry was adjourned for the attendance of the landlady, who, it was said, had met with an accident.

The unfortunate bride was born Margaret Elizabeth Lofty, the daughter of a deceased clergyman, who had been scratching a meagre living acting as companion to a series of elderly ladies. Her family were surprised to receive a letter on 17 December 1914 telling them that she had married John Lloyd, 'A thorough Christian man I have known since June', and now, only a few days later, she was dead.

By coincidence the paragraph in the paper was seen by Charles Burnham of Aston Clinton and Joseph Crossley in Blackpool, who both remarked on the similarity of Margaret Lofty's death to that of Alice Burnham. Unknown to one another, the two men both contacted the police, who started enquiries and Superintendent H. Wooton, of the Aylesbury police, wrote to Scotland Yard enclosing the cuttings that Mr Burnham had sent to him, including one from his local paper dated December 1913, which read:

Mrs George Smith, of 80, Kimberley Road, Portsmouth, who was married only six weeks ago, died suddenly at a Blackpool boarding house. Her husband, giving evidence at the inquest said he was of independent means. He met his wife, who was a nurse, three months ago and six weeks ago they were married. Last Wednesday, they travelled to Blackpool and engaged rooms at 16, Regent Road. During the journey, his wife complained of a headache and as she was no better on arrival, she saw a doctor. On Friday night, she took a hot bath. She was a considerable time in the bath and he called to her. There was no answer. He entered the bathroom and found his wife lying in the water, dead. Dr Billing said that a post-mortem showed that the heart was enlarged and affected. He concluded that the heat of the water had acted on the heart and caused either a fit or a faint and in her helplessness she was drowned.

It did not take the police long to discover that John Lloyd and George Joseph Smith were one and the same and on 1 February 1915 Smith was arrested while visiting a solicitor in Shepherd's Bush, seeking probate of Margaret's will.

The case immediately caught the attention of the public and the famous Edward Marshall Hall KC was inveigled into taking Smith's defence, finding out too late that because Smith had no money he would have to conduct the case within the terms of the Poor Person's Defence Act. This meant that for nine days' work at the trial he would receive the magnificent sum of £3 5s 6d, as legal etiquette dictated that once he had accepted the case he could not withdraw. Smith's solicitor, Mr W.D. Davies, had done a deal with a newspaper such that they would fund Smith's defence in return for the story of his life, signed by the accused, but this arrangement was vetoed by the Home Office as contrary to public policy – much to Marshall Hall's indignation.

The trial began at the Old Bailey on Tuesday 27 June 1915, in front of Mr Justice Scrutton and a packed public gallery. Technically, Smith was being tried for the murder of Bessie Mundy alone, but despite a spirited plea from Marshall Hall that no evidence should be heard regarding the other two deaths, the judge ruled that such evidence could be taken to show system. Throughout the hearing Smith frequently interrupted the proceedings as witness after witness went into the box to give damaging evidence against him.

The seventh day of the trial was almost entirely taken up with the evidence of Drs William Henry Willcox and Bernard Spilsbury, the latter basking in his burgeoning reputation after his appearance at the trial of Dr Crippen in 1910. They were questioned closely by Marshall Hall, who for once made little headway against two experienced practitioners, and the three baths used to drown the 'brides' were brought into the court as exhibits, much to the delight of the public gallery. Smith did not go into the witness box and in possibly one of the shortest submissions in a murder case ever heard at the Old Bailey, Marshall Hall confined his closing remarks largely to protesting about the admission of evidence regarding the other two murders, and the practice of using expert medical witnesses to contradict evidence already given by other medical men who were also the Crown's own witnesses. Mr Justice Scrutton summed up carefully, despite being interrupted several times by Smith, who at one time shouted 'Get on; hang me at once and have done with it, I am not a murderer, though I may be a bit peculiar!' The jury retired at 2.48 p.m. on the ninth day, 1 July 1915, and were back in court with a 'Guilty' verdict within twenty-two minutes. Smith was sentenced to death. After an appeal was turned down on 29 July he was carried to the scaffold, semi-conscious, by hangman John Ellis, assisted by Thomas Pierrepoint, on 13 August at Maidstone, protesting his innocence the while.

5

THE MAN FROM
THE PRU

Liverpool, 1931

The thousands of fans who visit Liverpool Football Club's Anfield stadium each week during the season probably neither know nor care that when they are cheering their team on, they are within half a mile of the scene of one of the greatest murder mysteries in English criminal history. It is a story that has everything – murder, suspense, fiendish planning and a plot that Agatha Christie would have been proud of. Even the judge who presided over the trial later commented, 'It was almost unexampled in the annals of crime.'

William Herbert Wallace was 52 years old, tall – looking taller by virtue of the bowler hat that he always wore outdoors – with wispy, receding grey hair, a straggly moustache and a cigarette never far from his lips, despite an infection that had resulted in the loss of one kidney and continued to give him problems. He and his wife Julia had lived at 29 Wolverton Street, Anfield, only 500 yards from the football ground, for the past sixteen years, happily so far as anyone could make out. The street was closed to motor traffic at the top end, although pedestrians could pass freely, and a single gas lamp halfway down provided flickering illumination at night. No. 29 was outwardly indistinguishable from thousands of similar terraced properties in the area, built on a three-up and three-down basis – plus a small back yard – and having the luxury of a bathroom and inside lavatory. At the back of each row of houses ran a narrow passageway, known locally as a 'back jigger', which also gave access to the street halfway down the row and which the Anfield residents used as a short cut, their comings and goings safe from the eyes of prying neighbours.

Wallace worked for the Prudential Assurance Company as a collection agent, his territory being the neighbouring area of Clubmoor. He visited more than 500 houses a week, mainly to collect premiums usually amounting to little more than two shillings a week, in what the Prudential referred to as the 'Industrial Branch'. The more remunerative 'Ordinary Branch' policies had

Julia Wallace, in happier days. (Author's collection)

premiums collected monthly.) He dabbled in chemistry and had set up a small laboratory in the tiny third bedroom at no. 29, his other main interest being chess. He also claimed to read the works of Marcus Aurelius and considered himself something of a stoic.

Julia Wallace was also 52, but looked older. She was a small, mousy woman, passing through the menopause and slightly incontinent, for which reason she wore a home-made diaper or nappy underneath her clothes. Sex, so far as Julia was concerned, was a thing of the past. She had few interests other than her piano, which she played well, sometimes accompanying her husband as he struggled with his violin lessons: these occasions must have been a mixed blessing for the neighbours, the Holmeses at no. 27 and the Johnstons at no. 31.

William Herbert Wallace.
(Author's collection)

Through this door in North John Street, W.H. Wallace walked down to the Central Chess Club in Cottle's City Café on the night before the murder. (Author)

Cottle's City Café, situated in a basement off North John Street in the business area of Liverpool, was the meeting place of the Liverpool Central Chess Club, which met on Monday and Thursday evenings. At about 7 p.m. on Monday 19 January 1931, Samuel Beattie, a cotton broker's manager and captain of the Chess Club, walked into the café and nodded a greeting to Gladys Harley, the waitress on duty. To the left of the entrance door was a telephone kiosk with '3581 Bank' painted on it and to the right, a noticeboard which was used by the club to display details of their competitions. That evening, according to the list, William Wallace was to play Mr F.C. Chandler in the Second Class Championship.

Beattie hung up his hat and coat and was beginning to prepare the room for the evening's matches when the telephone rang. It was answered by Gladys, who gestured to him and mouthed, 'It's for you.' A man's voice said, 'I would like to speak to Mr Wallace.' Beattie glanced round, but it was too early for any of the members to have arrived and he asked the caller if he would ring back later. 'I can't wait,' said the voice. 'I have my daughter's twenty-first on and I want to do something for her in the way of his business. Can you ask him to call on me tomorrow evening at 7.30. My name is R.M. Qualtrough and I live at 25 Menlove Gardens East, Mossley Hill.' Beattie promised that he would do his best to see that Wallace got the message, and at around 7.40 he noticed that Wallace had arrived and was settling down to a game with a Mr McCartney, Mr Chandler having failed to arrive. 'There's been a telephone call for you, Mr Wallace,' he said, and passed on the details. 'Qualtrough,' muttered Wallace. 'I don't know anyone of that name, and where is Menlove Gardens East?' Beattie, who lived in Mossley Hill, was unsure, but he thought that Menlove Gardens West came out in Menlove Avenue and another member of the club, Mr Deyes, agreed. Going home that evening with two of his friends, Wallace brought up the subject again. Neither of his companions was sure of the way but Wallace grunted, 'I've got a tongue in my head, I can enquire. Anyway, I'm not certain that I shall go.'

The next evening at about 6.45 Wallace walked down the yard of 29 Wolverton Street and let himself out by the back gate. Julia, who usually followed to bar the gate behind him, was suffering from a bad cold and stayed inside. His journey was to take three trams, the first of which left from the junction of Belmont Road and West Derby Road, a few minutes' walk away from his house, heading south along Shiel Road towards the junction of Lodge Lane and Smithdown Road. The second tram took him in a south-easterly direction, down Smithdown Road towards Penny Lane and the Mossley Hill area. No one noticed Wallace on the first tram, but on the second he asked the conductor, Thomas Phillips, no fewer than three times to be sure to put him off at Menlove Gardens East, as he had important business there. Phillips told him that the tram did not go that far, but he would be able to catch one of several trams going in that direction from Penny Lane. Arthur Thompson, conductor on the third tram – the no. 7 from Penny Lane to Calderstones – also remembered Wallace asking to be put off at Menlove Gardens East. 'When the car arrived at Menlove Gardens West,' he said later, 'I showed him the entrance to the road and said that he would probably find Menlove Gardens East in that direction.' The time was about 7.20.

During the next forty-five minutes, Wallace wandered about the area looking for R.M. Qualtrough, but although he found Menlove Gardens North, South and West, he could find no Menlove Gardens East. He stopped

Menlove Gardens South, looking towards Menlove Gardens North. (Author)

a young man, Sydney Green, who was coming down 'West', who told him that there was no such road as 'East'. Undeterred, Wallace knocked on the door of 25 Menlove Gardens West, the home of Mrs Katie Mather, who confirmed that there were only the three roads, and definitely no 'East'. A puzzled Wallace remembered that his superintendent at the Prudential, Joseph Crewe, lived on Green Lane, only a few minutes' walk away; but when he got to the house it was in darkness and no one answered the door. Retracing his steps, he encountered PC James Serjeant, who suggested that he might try at the local post office. When no one there was able to help he called at the newsagent's shop on nearby Allerton Road, where manageress Lily Pinches finally managed to convince him that he was on a fool's errand. By now thoroughly alarmed, he started on his journey home.

At about 8.45 Wallace's next-door neighbours, Mr and Mrs Johnston, were getting ready to go out. They used the back gate, as was their usual habit, and met Wallace walking down the passage-way towards his own back door. 'Have you heard anything unusual tonight?' he asked them, and explained that he was having difficulty gaining access to his house. 'The front door is locked against me,' he told them. 'And the back door won't open, either.' 'Try our key,' said Mr Johnston, and they waited while their neighbour walked up to the back door. 'It opens now,' said Wallace. 'We'll wait here until you check,' said Mr Johnston and Wallace vanished inside. They saw the gas lamp turned

The backyard door of 29 Wolverton Street,
where Wallace met Mr and Mrs Johnston
on the fatal evening. (Author)

up in the middle bedroom and also in the back kitchen. After a minute or so, Wallace reappeared and said urgently, 'Come and see. She has been killed.'

The Johnstons followed him into the back kitchen, along the hall and into the front parlour. By the light of a single gas lamp to the right of the fireplace, they could see Julia's body lying diagonally across the room, her feet in the fireplace and her head pointing towards the door. Spreading out from her head was an ominous halo of blood. 'Look at the brains,' said Wallace, bending down over the body. 'And what is she lying on? Why, it's a mackintosh, and my mackintosh!'

The police arrived, summoned by Mr Johnston, and were quickly followed by the photographer from the Liverpool Daily Post, who doubled as the police photographer. Next to arrive, just before 10 o'clock, was John Edward MacFall, Professor of Forensic Medicine at Liverpool University and Examiner in Medical Jurisprudence at no fewer than four other universities.

Wolverton Street. (Author)

He made a cursory examination of the body but did not trouble to take its temperature, which was unfortunate as temperature is an important factor in the determination of approximate time of death. Julia had been battered about the head several times with a hard instrument, the heaviest blow being just in front of the left ear, severing the meningeal artery. 'In my opinion,' MacFall announced, 'this lady has been dead for about four hours.' If he were right, it would mean that Julia had been killed before Wallace left for Menlove Gardens. Further examination of the body revealed that Julia's skirt was badly scorched down the front and that the mackintosh, which appeared to have been shoved underneath her shoulder, was similarly damaged and also blood-spattered. Julia must have fallen across the gas fire when she was attacked, although the fire was not lit when Wallace and the Johnstons entered the room.

Detective Superintendent Hubert Moore arrived and, after speaking briefly to the Johnstons, asked Wallace to show him round the house. The bedding in the front bedroom looked to have been disturbed, although Wallace was unable to account for it. 'I don't think I've been in here for a fortnight,' he told Moore. In the middle bedroom Wallace pointed to an ornament containing a few £1 notes. 'Here is some money that has not been touched,' he said, although later one of the notes was found to be slightly bloodstained. The remainder of the house was in order, with the exception of a cupboard in the back kitchen that had its door hanging off. A small cashbox lay on top of a bookcase to the left of the fireplace; Wallace said there was about £4 missing from it. A closer examination of the house by the police later disclosed a tiny clot of blood on the lavatory pan in the upstairs bathroom, although no other traces of blood were found apart from those in the front parlour.

Towards midnight Wallace was taken down to the main police station where he gave a statement, the final sentence before his signature reading, 'I have no suspicion of anyone', and finally a police car took him to the flat of his sister-in-law, Amy Wallace, at 83 Ullet Road, where he slept fitfully for what remained of the night. Over the next few days, the police continued their investigations, led by Detective Inspector Herbert Gold. The Wallaces' cleaning lady, Jane Sarah Draper, told the police that there was a thin poker missing, about 9in long, which usually lay in the kitchen fireplace, and a piece of iron used for cleaning under the gas fire was also missing from the parlour.

Then came an amazing development. The supervisor at the Anfield telephone exchange reported the logging of a call to Bank 3581, the number of the City Café, on the night before the murder. She was able to tell the police that the caller had had difficulties and although she at first suspected that he was trying to get a free call, she eventually put him through. The caller was ringing from Anfield 1627, and later in the day a telephone engineer confirmed that this number was that of a public telephone box on a triangle of ground at the junction of Breck Road and Priory Road, barely 400 yards from Wolverton Street. It was the only free-standing box in the area, all the others being on enclosed premises, and the police soon realised that the tram stop for North John Street was only a few steps away from it. Wallace (if it were he) could easily have made the call and then boarded the tram that would take him to the Chess Club.

Police enquiries showed that there were only six people with the name Qualtrough in the Liverpool telephone book, but none could throw any light on events. Over the next few days, groups of policemen travelled on the route which Wallace claimed to have taken, and became known as 'The Anfield Harriers' for their pains. These somewhat unsatisfactory 'tram tests' showed that Wallace could not have left his house much later than 6.49 p.m. on the first stage of his journey. Several people who were in the vicinity of Wolverton Street on the night of the murder were questioned by the police, including 13-year-old Elsie Wright, who told them that she had been helping 16-year-old Alan Close to deliver milk and that Close claimed to have seen Mrs Wallace at 6.45 on the night of the murder. If this was so, then Wallace would have an almost cast-iron alibi.

James Allison Wildman, a newspaper boy delivering papers at no. 27, confirmed Elsie's story but estimated that he saw Close standing on the doorstep of 29 Wolverton Street at about 6.37. The man who delivered the evening paper to the Wallace house said that he did so at around 6.35; this newspaper was later found by the police open on the kitchen table. There was now conflicting evidence as to the time Julia Wallace had been seen taking in the milk, but if Close was correct, Wallace would simply not have had the time to batter his wife to death, clean up and then catch the second tram down Smithdown Road at 7.10.

The inquest into Julia Wallace's death was opened and then immediately postponed. The Liverpool papers were full of the story, which soon caught the attention of the nationals, and Wolverton Street became thronged with reporters and photographers seeking any information they could find about the Wallaces. In the excitement, a young boy climbed over the back yard wall of no. 29 and was promptly ejected by the constable on duty.

In 70 per cent of domestic murder cases, the killer is the surviving spouse and Wallace was by now very firmly in the frame for the murder of his wife. A plain-clothes detective was sent to shadow him and at about 10.20 p.m. on 22 January, at the tram stop near the City Café, he saw Wallace greet Samuel Beattie, who was just on his way home from the Chess Club with another member, James Caird. The detective heard Wallace ask Beattie if he could be more certain about the time of the phone call on the Monday evening. 'Seven or shortly after,' was the reply. 'Cannot you get it nearer than that?' Wallace persisted. 'I'm sorry, but I cannot,' replied Beattie. 'I have just left the police,' said Wallace, 'and they have cleared me.'

On 2 February Superintendent Moore visited Amy Wallace's flat and arrested Wallace, charging him with Julia's murder. He was permitted to call a solicitor and chose Hector Munro, a fellow member of the Chess Club, although he did not know Munro personally. The committal proceedings opened on 19 February. Wallace was represented by Sidney Scholfield Allen, a young and promising barrister but relatively inexperienced in criminal cases. To the surprise of the defence it became clear that Alan Close had changed his story, and he now told the court that he saw Julia alive at 6.31 p.m., fourteen minutes earlier than his original statement. If this latter time were correct, Wallace would have had around eighteen minutes to commit the crime and get to his first tram stop – a very different proposition.

Professor MacFall was still of the opinion that Julia had been dead for about four hours when he first examined her, based on the progression of rigor mortis. This usually starts within five hours of death and appears first on the eyelids and lower jaw, spreading to the shoulders, arms and legs. It is fully established after around twelve hours, disappearing within twenty-four to thirty-six hours in the same order in which it started. However, its progress may be affected by the ambient temperature and by the physical attributes of the body concerned. The muscles of a well-built man will stiffen much later than those of a feeble elderly woman, and MacFall reluctantly admitted under examination that he could have been as much as an hour out either way in his estimate. He also admitted that the blood clot on the lavatory pan was most likely to have been carried there by one of the investigating team and had nothing to do with the murderer.

Reserving his defence, Wallace was committed to the Liverpool Spring Assizes and the question of defence costs now loomed; Hector Munro estimated that a sum in the region of £1,000 would be needed, nearly three times Wallace's annual salary. After careful consideration, including the holding of what amounted to a mock trial, the Prudential Staff Union agreed to meet the full cost of their colleague's defence and it was decided to brief Roland Oliver KC, a very experienced man who had already appeared in several notorious cases including Rex v. Steinie Morrison (1911), Thompson and Bywaters (1922) and Madame Fahmy (1923).

The trial opened on 22 April in the imposing surroundings of the neo-classical St George's Hall, Liverpool, Mr Justice Wright presiding. Leading for the Crown was Edward Hemmerde, Recorder of Liverpool, a man with a somewhat chequered career: a failed politician, a divorcé, and with a history of debts. The prosecution's case was that Wallace was the killer, that he had used the iron bar now said to be missing from the fireplace and that he had committed the crime while naked but for the mackintosh, which he had used to shield himself against the blood.

Samuel Beattie faced a gruelling time in the witness box, but kept his nerve. Oliver asked him whether he knew the accused man well and, when the answer was in the affirmative, took a huge gamble, ignoring the lawyer's first rule of never asking a question to which the answer is not known. Referring to the voice of R.M. Qualtrough, he asked, 'Does it occur to you now that it was anything like Wallace's voice?' The court held its breath before Beattie replied, 'It would be a great stretch of the imagination for me to say it was anything like that.'

Alan Close proved to be a difficult witness. Obviously nervous in the imposing surroundings and sulking at times, he gave his answers in a voice that the judge often found inaudible. He stuck to his revised story of seeing Julia at 6.31 p.m., having noticed the clock at Holy Trinity Church showing 6.25 as he walked along Richmond Park towards Wolverton Street, a journey that took about four to five minutes. He further claimed not to be able to recall any conversation with his friends about the time having been 6.45. The room buzzed when PC James Edward Rothwell told the court that he knew Wallace well and that on the afternoon of 20 January he saw him '. . . looking very distressed. He was dabbing his eye with his coat sleeve and it appeared that he had been crying.'

On the second day of the trial the Johnstons gave evidence of their meeting with Wallace and the discovery of the body. A locksmith, James Sarginson, deposed that the front door lock of 29 Wolverton Street was defective, although there was no indication that it had been damaged recently; and that the back door lock was rusty, and in good working order, although it required pressure to open it.

Then Professor MacFall once again stated his opinion that the time of death was nearer 6 o'clock than 7, despite the fact that this flew in the face of the evidence given by Alan Close. He went on to claim that the crime was committed 'in a frenzy', at which the public gallery buzzed excitedly until suppressed by the judge. The mackintosh was produced in evidence and the court was shown the burn marks and the bloodstains. MacFall admitted that even if Wallace had committed the crime wearing it, it would have been

The clock of Holy Trinity Church, Anfield, which Alan Close said he passed at 6.25 p.m. on 20 January. (Author)

difficult for him to avoid being splattered with blood, traces of which were found on the parlour walls up to a height of 4ft. The professor claimed to have no knowledge of the burn marks on Julia's skirt, which called into question the efficiency of his post-mortem examination, and then changed his evidence from what he had told the earlier court by claiming that the blood clot on the lavatory pan was carried there by the murderer. Superintendent Moore wound up the second day by implying that Wallace could not have entered the front parlour in the dark to light the gas lamp without tripping over Julia's body, unless he already knew that it was there and thus was able to avoid it.

The next morning Oliver, taking up the defence, pointed out to the court that Wallace 'is fifty-two, a delicate, mild man, liked by everyone who knows him, a man of considerable education and refinement'. He went on to stress that there was no evidence of any ill-feeling between the accused and his late wife; that he had nothing to gain from her death; that there was no suggestion of another woman; neither was there any evidence that he made the mysterious phone call on Monday evening, nor that he had enough time to commit the crime and then leave for Menlove Gardens, unflustered and with not a speck of blood on him. Finally, despite an extensive search, no murder weapon had been found.

Wallace answered Oliver's questions calmly and said that he made upwards of 560 calls a week in the course of his business. Three weeks out of four the weekly take was between £30 and £40, but in every fourth week it might be anything between £80 and £100 or even more. In the week of the murder he had collected around £14, most of which he had paid out in sickness benefits; he confirmed without hesitation that he had used the Breck Road telephone box on occasion, but that no one had ever left a message for him at the Chess Club before. In reply to a question about the kind of business he might envisage doing at Menlove Gardens, he said, 'I considered it might result in a policy of something like £100 endowment . . . I did not expect that it would be less than that.' (Wallace could have expected to receive commission of 20 per cent of the first annual premium, with repeat commission of a smaller sum throughout the life of the policy.) 'Did you lay a finger on her?' asked Oliver. 'Did you lay a hand upon your wife at all, that night?' Misunderstanding the question Wallace answered, 'I think, in going out of the back door, I did what I often enough did. I just patted her on the shoulder and said I won't be any longer than I can help.' 'Is there anyone in the world who could take the place of your wife in your life?' Oliver asked. 'No, there is not.' 'Have you got anyone to live with now?' 'No.'

The following day, a Saturday, Oliver and Hemmerde made their closing speeches and the judge summed up – if anything slightly in favour of the accused, cautioning the jury that they must be satisfied beyond reasonable doubt before returning a guilty verdict. Precisely one hour later, the jury

An accused's-eye view of the judge's chair in the courtroom at St George's Hall, taken from the dock, where both Florence Maybrick and William Wallace went on trial for their lives. (Author)

returned and to the astonishment of most people in the court, pronounced Wallace guilty. The judge donned the black cap and without further comment sentenced Wallace to death. 'I am not guilty,' said Wallace, 'I don't want to say anything else', before disappearing down the steps to the cells.

It was decided to appeal and, although several points were made, the only ground that had any real chance of success was that the verdict was unreasonable and against the weight of the evidence. The appeal was heard over two days, 18 and 19 May, with the panel of judges led by the Lord Chief Justice, Lord Hewart of Bury. In the early afternoon of 19 May their lordships retired to consider their verdict and were back within the hour. Lord Hewart began his judgment by pointing out that this was a case of doubt and difficulty and that the judges were not concerned with suspicion, however grave, or with theories, however ingenious. 'Section 4 of the Criminal Appeal Act of 1907,' he said slowly, 'provides that the Court of Criminal Appeal shall allow the appeal if they think that the verdict of the jury should be set aside on the ground that it cannot be supported having regard to the evidence. The conclusion at which we have arrived is that the case against the appellant . . . is not proved with that certainty which is necessary in order to justify a verdict of guilty, and, therefore . . . the result is that this appeal will be allowed and the conviction quashed.' Wallace, looking bewildered and almost certainly unaware that this was the first time that a guilty verdict in a capital murder case had been overturned in such a way, walked from the court a free man. In due course he attempted to go back to his old job, but the people of Clubmoor were edgy and in some cases downright hostile, and he quickly realised that this was not an option. He could no longer bear to stay in the tiny house in Wolverton Street and moved to a bungalow on the Wirral, the removal firm noting that the parlour walls at no. 29 were still heavily spattered with blood as described to the author by one of the removal men, who was still alive in the 1970s.

Shortly after the murder the police received a fifteen-page handwritten letter, now with the trial papers at the National Archives, headed 'The Great Wallace Mystery: Should The Murder Have Been Solved', written by Robert Carr of Lodge Lane, Liverpool, who claimed that on the night of the murder a man and a woman approached him in Scotland Road at about 8.10 asking for directions to the landing stage at the Pier Head. The man, so Carr insisted, bore a resemblance to a picture of Wallace that had appeared in the Empire News. Carr followed up his letter with a series of requests for interviews with everyone from Inspector Gold to the Chief Constable. He was politely but firmly fobbed off by the CID. The Central Police Office, Liverpool, later confirmed to the Home Office that at least three people had confessed to the murder, one anonymously. The police made it clear that they were not looking for anyone else in connection with Julia's death.

For the next two years Wallace led a lonely life, commuting each day to a desk job at the Prudential headquarters in Liverpool, before succumbing to an infection in his remaining kidney and dying in Clatterbridge Hospital on 26 February 1933. He was buried in Anfield Cemetery in the same grave as Julia. The Daily Express published a note of his estate – gross £1,614, net £620. The matter might well have ended there if Jonathan Goodman, in his definitive book The Killing of Julia Wallace, published in 1969, had not referred to a list, given by Wallace to the police, of people whom his wife would unhesitatingly have admitted to the house in his absence. Among about a dozen names were Superintendent Crewe, James Caird and his family, Wallace's music teacher Mr Davis and a Richard Gordon Parry.

Parry, aged about 22 at the time of the murder, had worked for the Prudential at one time and had once done Wallace's round for him for a few days when the latter was in bed with influenza. He came from a good family, his father being a treasury official with Liverpool Corporation, and was at the time of the murder working for another insurance company in the area.

Police 'mug shot' of Richard Gordon Parry, taken several years after the death of Julia Wallace. (Richard Whittington-Egan)

Wallace claimed that Parry was well acquainted with the workings of his household and also that he had seen him at the City Café about three months before the murder. He also told the police that although it was not generally known, Parry had withheld some of the premium monies he had collected while working for the Prudential and Mr Crewe had eventually gone to his parents, who made up the sum of about £30.*

Goodman discovered that late on the night of the murder Parry, driving a motor car, called into a garage on Moscow Drive, about a mile from Wolverton Street as the crow flies, and insisted that the boy on duty – John Parkes, a poorly educated lad employed merely to serve petrol – should hose his car down, inside and out. He explained to the impressionable Parkes that he knew something about the Wallace murder, news of which had already

---

* Had this been true, it is almost certain that Parry would have been dismissed out of hand, and it would have been extremely unlikely that he would have been able to find a job with another insurance company afterwards.

spread like wildfire throughout the area. Showing the boy a pair of gloves that he claimed were soaked in blood, he told him that if the police were to find out, 'It would hang me.' A few days later, Parkes told this story to his employers, who insisted that he should inform the authorities at once. Parry was interviewed but was able to satisfy the police that he had an alibi and that he had just been joking with Parkes, whom he knew was not very bright. This alibi was supposed to have been provided by his then girlfriend, Lily Lloyd; two years later, having fallen out with Parry, she went to Hector Munro and retracted her story. By then Wallace was dead and Munro took no further action, but in any case, Parry's alibi for the time of the murder had been provided by someone else and did not rely on the girl's testimony.

The 'back jigger' running behind 29 Wolverton Street, showing the rectangular 'midden' doors where Wallace could have disposed of the murder weapon. (Author)

In 1966 Goodman and fellow crime-writer Richard Whittington-Egan traced Parry and had a short interview with him, during which he claimed that in Wallace's absence he had frequently visited Wolverton Street, where Julia dispensed tea and accompanied his singing on the piano. Even today, visitors to Wolverton Street soon discover that conversations in the front rooms of the little houses can be heard quite clearly from the street – the age of double glazing apparently not yet having reached this part of Liverpool. In addition the connecting walls between the terraced houses are thin, and the sound of musical afternoons while the man of the house was absent would very quickly have been the talk of the street – as would the furtive afternoon visits of a young man. The idea that there was something going on between Parry and the ageing, incontinent Julia is risible and this suggestion by Parry shows that he was indeed the sort of young man who would have lost no opportunity to tease the uneducated Parkes, and who was also quite prepared to tell equally tall stories to Goodman and his companion, no doubt laughing up his sleeve as he did so.

When Goodman's book was published, he could not name Parry as his prime suspect for legal reasons, merely describing him as 'Mr X', but when Parry died on 16 December 1980 it then became possible to reveal his name as the suspected murderer. It was known that Parry had a minor criminal record, acquired some years after the Wallace case, and in 1981 Liverpool's Radio City ran two programmes on the case in which Parry was accused outright of the murder. The producer of the programme, Roger Wilkes, later published his own book on the case, Wallace – The Final Verdict, which repeated the story and featured what was obviously a police 'mug shot' of Parry, taken a few years after the Wallace case. Since then most other authors dealing with the case have included the Parry connection and have concluded that he was the killer.

In the author's view, this is unfortunate and maligns a man who was obviously not guilty of the crime, as not only did he have a cast-iron alibi for the time of the murder, but the story of his secret liaison with Julia is patently ridiculous. Whatever minor misdemeanours Parry may have committed in later life, he did not deserve to be saddled with the murder of Julia Wallace and if he is removed from the scene, the only other candidate is Wallace himself. Whoever killed Julia had only a very short time in which to commit the crime, tidy up and leave the house, taking with him whatever weapon was used. Ludicrous though it may seem, it might well have been an eminently practical precaution to commit the murder wearing a raincoat, naked underneath or not, and with luck avoid any splashes of blood. That the weapon was never found is hardly surprising – every house in the area had a midden, or ash-pit, which the Liverpool Corporation workforce emptied each week via a small wooden door in the outside back yard wall. It would have been the work of seconds for the murderer to open one of hundreds of such middens in the area and to plunge the weapon deep into the ashes inside, to be disposed of unknowingly by the Corporation a few days later. In addition there were hundreds of acres of open space in the Anfield area where the weapon could have been safely hidden as the murderer hurried away. However, he would have had no reason to remove it and thus risk getting contaminated by the blood-soaked weapon unless it was of such a nature that it could have been traced back directly to him.*

Although Wallace claimed that he was a stranger to the Menlove Gardens area, he had visited Superintendent Crewe at his house in Green Lane on at least five occasions, and from the top end of Green Lane the entrance to Menlove Gardens North is clearly visible, likewise the entrance to Menlove Gardens West from Menlove Avenue itself, as the tram conductor pointed out on the fatal evening. In addition Calderstones Park is only a matter of a hundred yards from Green Lane and Wallace had certainly taken Julia there on more than one occasion, as his diaries disclosed, so he would have had several opportunities to walk along the 'Gardens' while visiting the area. One also has to wonder why the mysterious Mr Qualtrough should have chosen Menlove Gardens if he really wanted to lure Wallace away on the Tuesday evening. The journey was an awkward one to make in the middle of winter and there were plenty of other addresses which might have been more attractive to an insurance man seeking commission income and which would have taken him away from Wolverton Street long enough for the crime to be committed.

Time is obviously of the essence in this case and if Alan Close's amended estimate of the time that he saw Julia at her front door was correct, Wallace would have had long enough to commit the murder and be on his way. To be fair to Wallace, Holy Trinity Church clock could have been a couple of minutes fast or slow, and when Close looked at it on his way down Richmond Park he can have had no idea that an accurate reading was to be so vital. In addition, although Wallace's three trams were listed on the timetable to depart at certain times, no evidence was given at the trial that they actually departed when the timetable said they did. Even Professor MacFall's estimate of the time of death was rendered useless

---

* It was never mentioned in court, but it would have been surprising if Wallace's upstairs laboratory had not contained a retort stand, consisting of a heavy metal base into which an iron rod was screwed to support his experiments. It would have been the work of seconds to unscrew the rod and use it to beat Julia about the head, but as only Wallace would have known its whereabouts, it would have been vital to remove this piece of incriminating evidence.

by his failure to take the temperature of the body when he arrived on the scene. Determination of time of death even now, over seventy years later, is still fraught with difficulty and most modern pathologists would hesitate before giving estimates within an hour either way. MacFall's assessment that Julia had been dead four hours, without even taking the temperature, was irresponsible and served only to muddy the waters.

Finally, the motive. While there was no evidence that Wallace and his wife did not get on, Julia was ailing and had long since gone to seed; her clothes were dowdy and old-fashioned and she shared few of her husband's interests. Wallace, not in the best of health himself, visited households where for the most part the husband was out at work and, aside from the collection of premiums, it was also his responsibility to pay out on policies that matured – including those times when the man of the house had died leaving a sorrowing widow behind. Naturally Wallace would have been at his comforting best on those occasions, not least because his income depended on his being able to replace a maturing policy with a new one. The author believes that it is not inconceivable that Wallace and one of his recently bereaved clients began to grow close and the more he looked at Julia, the more attractive to him the idea of a liaison became; but when he ventured to broach the subject with the lady concerned, he was rebuffed. 'Ah, Herbert, if only you weren't married. . . .' From that moment, he decided that Julia would have to go and he began to plan her demise. Killing Julia was risky, of course, but if he could establish an alibi for himself that put him 5 miles from the scene of the crime, he might well get away with it. How was he to know about rigor mortis or estimations of time of death?

On the other hand, if Wallace was not Qualtrough, what possible motive was there for a convoluted plan which involved a mysterious phone call, a three-tram journey and the possibility that Julia would not admit the caller anyway? Qualtrough could just as well have done the deed on Monday night, when Wallace was out of the house for three hours at the chess club – a fact which could easily have been verified by a telephone call to the club once the members had arrived, say at around 8 o'clock. The caller could have rung off once he had ascertained that Wallace was in the club, without having to speak to him. Wallace, at the time of the murder and later, always insisted that Parry was dishonest while he was working for the Prudential and would surely have discussed this with Julia and given her instructions to have nothing to do with him should he ever call. Why then, in his statement to the police, did he describe Parry as 'a friend of my wife and myself?' One wonders whether it was possible that Parry's charade with Parkes somehow came to Wallace's attention and that he swiftly used this to throw suspicion on the other man.

The grave in Anfield Cemetery where
William and Julia lie together. (Author)

In the end, no one else was ever arrested for the crime and Parry's connection with it has proved to be a considerable red herring. He was certainly a liar and a petty criminal in later life, but he was innocent of murder; the real killer was William Herbert Wallace, killing for love and having luck with him on that cold night in January 1931.

6

RED STAINS ON THE CARPET

Lancaster, 1935

On the night of 15 October 1935 a four-seater Austin Twelve motor car drew into the side of the A701, two miles outside Moffat on the Edinburgh Road, its windscreen wipers struggling to cope with the rain. Although it was dark the driver knew where he was, as he had made this journey several times before, albeit in better weather and in daylight. On his right-hand side a 3ft brick wall protected a drop into a ravine, known locally as the Gardenholme Linn, in the bottom of which was a stream, usually narrow but now transformed into a torrent by the incessant rain that had been falling for more than twenty-four hours.

The driver got out, head down against the weather, and stumbled to the rear of his vehicle. Feeling for the boot catch in the darkness, he lifted the cover and reached inside. The bundle he brought out needed both hands to lift and it was with some difficulty that he carried the heavy load and dropped it over the wall. Over the howling of the wind he could not hear the noise as the parcel landed 40ft below, and in any case he was already groping into the car boot for another. After that came two more, and then he returned for the last time with a large bag which he perched on the wall and opened, dropping the contents to join the parcels below. Closing the boot, he got back into his car, panting with the effort. His hands were wet and greasy and he wiped them on a piece of rag before putting the key into the ignition. He was more than a hundred miles from home and it was late.

The county town of Lancaster has a long history, its castle on a commanding position overlooking the town dating back to Roman times, although the keep is Norman. Driving through the town via the A6 and heading south the motorist passes Dalton Square on the left, built mostly in the late eighteenth century and dominated by a statue of Queen Victoria in the middle. At 2 Dalton Square, a three-storey, double-fronted property, there lived in 1935

View of the bridge over the Gardenholme Linn where the remains were found.
(Edinburgh University Forensic Department)

36-year-old Dr Bukhtyar Rustomji Ratanji Hakim, a Bachelor of Medicine of the Universities of London and Bombay and a Bachelor of Surgery of the University of Bombay, although he had failed his English surgery examinations. He had lived in Dalton Square with his 'wife' Isabella (known to her husband as 'Belle' and actually a Mrs Van Ess), their three children and a succession of maids since 1930, during which time he had developed a substantial practice. Although Asian doctors were a rarity in those days, Hakim, who had anglicised his name to Buck Ruxton, was well regarded and popular. The current maid was a girl of just gone 20 named Mary Jane Rogerson, whose father and stepmother lived in Morecambe, 4 miles away. Mary was employed to look after the Ruxtons' three children; her stepmother helped her occasionally by repairing the children's clothing, and there was every reason to believe that Mary was happy in her work – although her worn shoes and jumble-sale clothes indicated that perhaps the job did not pay very well.

Ruxton was known as an excitable person, not above assaulting his wife and threatening her with knives, although these rages never lasted long and the making-up afterwards seemed to be thoroughly enjoyed by both of them. Despite this, Mrs Ruxton had gone into the police station at the Town Hall on the south side of the square at least twice in the past two years to complain to the police that her husband had accused her of unfaithfulness with other men and had struck her. The police had taken no action.

Dr and Mrs Ruxton with one of their children. (popperfoto.com)

The door of Dr Ruxton's house in Dalton Square, Lancaster. After his arrest it was never again used as a private residence. (Author)

Every year it was Mrs Ruxton's habit to meet her sisters, Mrs Nelson and Mrs Madden, and see the Blackpool Illuminations. Dr Ruxton had on more than one occasion accused her of using this trip as an opportunity to meet men, and only a week before she disappeared there had been another row when Isabella went to Scotland with a party of friends and stayed overnight at an Edinburgh hotel. Ruxton had followed her and accused her of having an illicit relationship with one of the young men in the party, Robert James Edmondson, an assistant solicitor in the Lancaster town clerk's department. The charge was completely unfounded. Although the Blackpool visit was sure to provide another opportunity for her husband to make more of these allegations, Mrs Ruxton insisted on going and went alone in her husband's car to see her sisters on Saturday 14 September 1935, returning in the early hours. Although the car was parked outside the house the following morning, no one apart from Dr Ruxton and the maid ever saw Isabella alive again.

Two days before, Ruxton had told his cleaner, Mrs Elizabeth Curwen, that as his wife and the maid were in Edinburgh there would be nothing for her to do and she need not come in again until the following Monday. The lady who did the rough work and some of the cooking, Mrs Agnes Oxley, was due to go into work on 15 September, but early in the morning her husband was surprised to receive a visit from the doctor, who said that his wife was away and that he was going to take the children to Morecambe for a day out. However, he did ask that Mrs Oxley should come in the following day. Later that same morning, the lady who delivered the newspapers knocked on the Ruxtons' front door and was surprised to find it opened by an agitated-looking Dr Ruxton, who seemed to be having a problem with his right hand, which he held close against his body. When the milk was delivered, he told the delivery girl that he had 'jammed his hand'.

Shortly before midday Ruxton and his children appeared at the Morecambe house of Mr and Mrs Anderson, friends who agreed to look after the children for the day, as the doctor said that he was busy and his wife and Mary Rogerson were away from home for a while. Mr Anderson noticed that the doctor had a very severe gash across three fingers of his right hand, one of which was cut to the bone, and Ruxton explained that the tin-opener had slipped that morning while he was opening a tin of peaches for breakfast. At 4.30 p.m. Ruxton visited a patient, Mrs Hampshire, and asked her to go back to Dalton Square with him and help, as he had cut his hand badly and was getting the house ready for the decorators. He explained that his wife was in Blackpool and that Mary Rogerson had gone away for a few days' holiday. When Mrs Hampshire arrived she found the house in some disarray, with uneaten meals on the table, straw littering the floors, and two of the bedroom doors locked. The bath was stained a nasty yellow colour almost up to the top and Ruxton requested that this should be cleaned especially thoroughly. In his waiting room, rolled-up carpet and some stair pads were lying on the floor, together with a man's suit; and there were other bits of carpet, heavily stained, in the back yard, all of which he told Mrs Hampshire to take away. At 7 p.m. the doctor arrived back at the house, having collected his children from the Andersons.

The following morning Ruxton turned up at the Hampshires, looking ill, and asked Mrs Hampshire if she would stand in for his charlady, who would not be able to go in that day. He then asked her for the suit back, saying that he had realised that it was too heavily soiled and would need cleaning before it could be worn again. Mrs Hampshire told him that as he had been kind enough to give her the suit, the least she could do would be to pay for the cleaning. Ruxton then insisted that a label inside the jacket, bearing his name, should be cut off and burnt immediately. When the doctor had gone Mrs Hampshire had a good look at the clothing and found that the suit, and in particular the waistcoat, was so badly stained that she could do nothing except burn it. The carpets were also heavily stained; she threw no fewer than thirty buckets of cold water on them in the back yard without being able to get them clean. The water that came off was the colour of blood.

When Ruxton returned to Dalton Square he found Mrs Oxley waiting for him; she went into the surgery and helped the doctor to bandage his injured hand. He then remarked that he thought that the visit to Edinburgh by his wife and the maid was a put-up job, and said that Mary Rogerson had asked for her wages before she left. When Mrs Hampshire arrived in response to Ruxton's request she found the doctor in a tearful state, moaning about his wife having a clandestine relationship with another man. In the early afternoon Ruxton took his car for servicing and rented a replacement vehicle for one and a half days, returning at 9.15 in the evening to the Andersons to arrange for the children to spend another night with them.

On the early afternoon of Tuesday 17 September he was involved in a motor accident in Kendal when he ran into a cyclist, Bernard Beattie, and knocked him off his bicycle. Beattie was only bruised, but the bicycle was wrecked. Ruxton failed to stop, but the shaken man had the presence of mind to write down the number of the car and at 1 p.m. it was stopped at Milnthorpe, a few miles south. In the car were Ruxton and his 2-year-old son, Billie. The doctor was very agitated and almost incoherent when approached by the policeman, denying having smashed up the bicycle, although he did admit that his car had been involved in an accident. He was told to produce his documents at Lancaster police station and sent on his way.

Returning to Dalton Square, he asked Mrs Curwen to build a large fire in the waiting room, as he was going to stay up all night. The next day, Mrs Curwen called at 8.30 a.m. and found a large quantity of burned material in the back yard, including some clothing that she thought had belonged to Mary Rogerson. By mid-afternoon Ruxton was back in Morecambe, where his eldest daughter Elizabeth was to take part in the annual carnival procession. The three children again stayed the night with the Andersons and Ruxton returned home to pick up his car after its service.

On Thursday 19 September Mrs Oxley heard Ruxton make several journeys up and down the stairs to his car, parked outside in the passageway. She could not see what he was doing and the door to his bedroom remained locked. The car drove off shortly after 8 a.m. and returned at 3 in the afternoon. After this all the rooms remained open and were not locked again, but there was a strange smell in Ruxton's own room (he and his wife had separate bedrooms), and on the following morning Ruxton sent Mrs Curwen out for a spray and a bottle of eau-de-cologne. In the afternoon, the doctor encountered young Mr Edmondson in the street and chatted amicably to him about Isabella. He enquired about Edmondson's professional examinations and told him that a small betting business that his wife had started had collapsed and that she and her sister were spending some time in London with another relative.

The following Monday Mrs Smith, who had been taken on only recently by Dr Ruxton, was doing the washing when she came across a nightgown with a large bloodstain on one shoulder; she washed it and hung it out to dry. In the evening Mary Rogerson's brother, Peter, called to enquire about his sister and was told that Mrs Ruxton had taken her on a fortnight's holiday. Ruxton then asked him whether he had heard anything about Mary going out with a laundry boy. Plainly puzzled, the young man took the 15s, which was Mary's weekly wage, and returned home. That evening Ruxton went to the cinema to see Clive of India.

An agitated Dr Ruxton visited the police station on 24 September and complained about a police interview with Mrs Curwen concerning the death of a Mrs Smalley in Morecambe, whose body had been found lying in a stable yard and who appeared to have been the victim of a hit-and-run driver. Why the police should have wished to question the cleaning lady is not clear, but the likely explanation is that they were interviewing all the car owners in the area and, as Dr Ruxton was not on the premises when the police called, they interviewed the person who answered the door. This interview appears to have been entirely innocuous and a matter of routine, but Ruxton was very upset about it and in the course of his conversation with the police he said that his wife had left him a fortnight previously, taking the maid with her, and that he had no idea of their whereabouts. The police, assuming that this was just one more of the Ruxtons' well-known 'spats', did not take it very seriously.

The following day he called on the Rogersons and told them that Mary had been 'different' in the past few weeks. She had been seeing a local laundry boy and was pregnant, so his wife had taken the girl away to get an abortion. The Rogersons were understandably upset at this amazing news; Mr Rogerson said that his daughter must be brought back, pregnant or not, and that he would report the matter to the police if she did not return by Saturday. On Thursday Ruxton told a friend that he suspected his wife of having an affair with young Edmondson and that she had left him, taking Mary Rogerson with her; and on the following Monday he again called on Mrs Hampshire to see if the suit had been cleaned, and joked with her about the Smalley case. The next evening the Rogersons called at Dalton Square and were told that Ruxton had no idea where the two women were, but they had taken money out of his safe and would no doubt come home when it ran out. They left, again telling the doctor that they would go to the police.

On the afternoon of 29 September a young Edinburgh tourist, Susan Haines Johnson, happened to be standing by the wall overlooking the Gardenholme Linn and noticed several bundles on the bank of the stream below, wrapped in white sheeting. To her horror, she saw sticking out of one of the bundles what looked very much like a human arm, so she hastily called to her brother, who climbed into the ravine to take a closer look. What he saw sent him running into Moffat for the police. When officers arrived at the Linn they found four bundles containing human remains, including two human heads, two arms

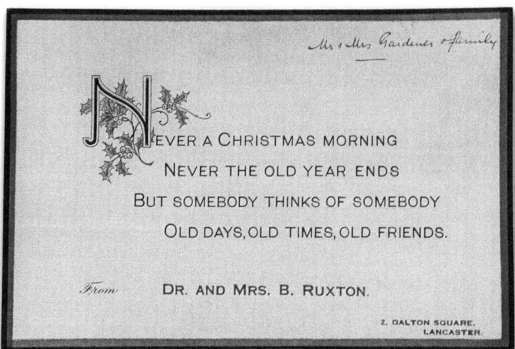

Christmas cards sent from the Ruxtons to Mr Gardner, the family solicitor. Note the reference on the first to 'Doctor Joy'. (Miss Joan Gardner)

complete with hands, a thigh bone and various pieces of flesh. The bundles lay on the left-hand bank about 6ft from the bridge, which was fortunate, for if the remains had been thrown a little to the right they might well have been washed downstream and out of sight, where decomposition, birds and wild animals would soon have resulted in their complete disappearance.

The first bundle was wrapped in a blouse, the second in a pillow slip, the third in a piece of cotton sheet and the fourth parcel was tied together with the hem from a cotton sheet. There were also pieces of newspaper dated 15 September. Altogether there were approximately seventy pieces of dismembered flesh and bone; both heads were wrapped in cotton wool and one was enclosed in a pair of child's rompers. The remains were all in a state of decomposition and infested with maggots. As the small mortuary at Moffat did not have the facilities necessary to handle the remains it was decided to remove them to the University of Edinburgh laboratories, where they were inspected by Dr David Huskie of Edinburgh University and Professor John Glaister from Glasgow. It quickly became clear that there were the remains of just two bodies and, while one of the heads had all the appearance of being female, the other one was at first thought to be male. The pieces were sorted and allocated to two boxes, labelled 'Body No. 1' and 'Body No. 2'. Dr James Brash, Professor of Anatomy at Edinburgh University, and his assistants took on the task of anatomical investigation, including reconstruction of the bodies and photographing the parts. More remains were found further down the Linn on 30 September, and 2 and 3 October, and on 28 October a roadman working on the Glasgow–Carlisle road about 9 miles south of Moffat found a rain-soaked newspaper parcel which contained a left foot. On 4 November a woman walking along the Edinburgh–Moffat road found a right forearm and hand wrapped in newspaper, about half a mile south of the Linn. Meanwhile, Chief Constable William Black of Dumfriesshire Constabulary, fearing that his small force would be out of their depth with this major investigation, sought the assistance of the Chief Constable of Glasgow, Captain P.J. Sillitoe, who was able to second various experts to the investigation. On 1 October the police issued a press statement to the effect that the person or persons responsible for the mutilation of the bodies might well have had some sort of anatomical knowledge, as an obvious attempt had been made to destroy any evidence that would lead to an early identification. Flesh had been cut away from some of the limbs, the heads were mutilated and several teeth had been extracted. Death was estimated to have taken place about ten days previously.

Dr Ruxton was back at the police station on 2 October to register his wife as a missing person and to complain that there were rumours going round the town connecting the disappearance of his wife and the maid with the bodies found in pieces up in Scotland. He claimed that one or two patients had left his panel and gone to other doctors, and the obviously nervous and emotional

Ruxton demanded that the police should issue a statement denying that he was involved with the incident. The police, who were by now beginning to wonder about the little Indian doctor, assured him that they would issue a statement when they had something to say. Ruxton replied that the police were welcome to search his house any time they wished.

Meanwhile, in the forensic laboratories at Edinburgh University the doctors continued their examination and gradually drew the pieces of the jigsaw together. Each part was allocated to a particular body, the 'female' head being placed with 'Body No. 1' and the other – which had now also been identified as female – with 'Body No. 2'. The latter was to a large extent complete, apart from a missing right foot, but 'Body No. 1' had the whole of the chest and abdominal area absent. These were never found; it is assumed that they were either washed down the ravine and into the River Annan, or dumped elsewhere. Pictures of the child's rompers and blouse were published in the press and enquiries were made of the printers of the newspaper that had been found with the remains. This turned out to be an issue of the Sunday Graphic and Sunday News, which was circulated only in the Lancaster and Morecambe area and the date of which coincided with the last day that Mrs Ruxton and her maid had been seen alive. Eventually Mrs Rogerson was able to identify the blouse and the child's rompers. She had sewn in a patch under one arm of the blouse before giving it to her stepdaughter, and she also told the police that a friend of the Ruxtons had given them some child's clothing, including the rompers. These were later positively identified by the donor.

On Friday 4 October Ruxton was again at the police station in a disturbed state, repeating his invitation to search the house and suggesting that his name was being associated with the murder of Mrs Smalley. His wife had left him on 15 September and he suggested that young Edmondson knew more about this than he was admitting to. His telephone bill had been excessive and there had been what he termed 'silly love-talk', although he did not say precisely how he knew this. On the Saturday Ruxton called on Mr Edmondson senior to ask where his son was, and accusations were made which so alarmed the father that when his son returned home later in the day, they decided that it would be as well to go to see Ruxton and sort things out once and for all.

On Sunday 6 October they saw the doctor and Robert Edmondson, known to his family as 'Bobbie', told Ruxton that he had not the faintest idea where Mrs Ruxton was. Edmondson senior made it quite clear to the doctor that if there were any more insinuations from him regarding an illicit affair between Bobbie and Ruxton's wife, legal proceedings would quickly follow. The following day Isabella's sister, Mrs Nelson, received a letter from Ruxton saying that Belle had left him once again and that she was heavily in debt. She was trying to help the maid, who was 'in trouble'; he said that he would come up to Edinburgh to discuss the matter further, but by this time Mrs Nelson was getting fed up with the hysterical doctor and declined to see him.

On Wednesday 9 October Mrs Rogerson finally made good her threat to go to the police and gave a description of her missing daughter for circulation. On the same day Ruxton went up to Edinburgh and saw Isabella's two sisters. He talked for a long time, although little of what he said made any sense and by then, of course, the newspapers were full of the story of the Gardenholme Linn and its grisly contents.

On his return from Edinburgh Ruxton was met at the railway station by Inspector Clark, and he told the policeman that Bobbie Edmondson knew the whereabouts of the two missing women, claiming that the young man and Isabella had stayed together at the Adelphi Hotel, Edinburgh, under the names of Mr and Mrs Ruxton. Later that day he visited Mrs Hampshire and again told her to burn the carpets and the suit. He then saw Detective Constable Winstanley at the police station and said, angrily, that he was still being associated with the remains found in Scotland. Several questions were asked of him regarding Mary Rogerson and her supposed pregnancy, and he gave permission for Isabella's description to be published by the police.

At 9.30 p.m. Ruxton was once more at the police station, clutching a copy of the Daily Express which referred to the teeth of one of the bodies. 'Look at this,' he cried. 'Why do they not accuse me of the Moffat murder? Someone will be putting a dead baby on my doorstep and I will be accused of killing it!' He then sought an interview with Mr Vann, the Chief Constable, complaining about the newspaper reports and claiming to know 'for a fact' that Mary Rogerson had at least four teeth missing on the lower jaw, whereas the newspaper report claimed that all the teeth were intact. The doctor was almost foaming at the mouth, and the Chief Constable had the greatest difficulty in understanding him when he went on to accuse Bobbie Edmondson of ruining his home and his marriage and to ask if the police could intercept letters in the post. He again asked if the police would publish a statement disassociating him from the two bodies up in Scotland – to which the Chief Constable gave a non-committal reply.

On 12 October Ruxton tried to contact as many of his friends and acquaintances as he could, to rehearse them in backing up the various stories that he had been putting out. He saw Mrs Oxley and attempted to persuade her to say that on the Sunday morning when he told her that she need not come to the house, she actually did go until 11 a.m. Confused and by now worried, Mrs Oxley said that she could not say that as it would not be true. In particular, he sought out Ernest Hall, an operator at a local cinema who had seen him on Saturday 14 September to get a sick note. Ruxton was keen to get him to say that the visit had actually been two days later, on the 16th, and that Mary Rogerson had opened the door to him – but Hall stoutly stuck by his story.

At 9.30 p.m. the doctor was summoned to the police station, where Vann told him that he was sure Ruxton could help the police in finding his wife and the maid; he wanted him to account for his movements between 14 and 26 September. To Vann's surprise Ruxton produced a handwritten document headed 'My Movements', covering the period from 14 to 30 September. He also made a statement, running to 4,500 words, which was really only an expanded version of 'My Movements'. In it he said that he and his wife had not slept together since the previous Christmas and that she had left the house on the morning of 15 September after getting back late from Blackpool. He said she had taken Mary Rogerson with her. He had refused to let her use his car and did not know where the two women were. The interview went on through the night, Vann taking down the doctor's statement in his own handwriting. At 7.20 a.m. on Sunday 13 October a tearful and exhausted Ruxton was arrested for the murder of Mary Rogerson, a charge that he hotly denied. He appeared at the Lancaster Police Court the following day to be remanded in custody, later being charged with the murder of his wife too, and he remained in the cells until 26 November when the case began to be heard.

Ruxton's family solicitor, Mr Charles Frederick Gardner, was held in high regard in Lancaster but had no experience in criminal matters and so Accrington solicitor Edwin Slinger took on the responsibility of acting for the accused man. On 13 December Ruxton was committed for trial at Manchester Assizes on charges of the murders of his wife and Mary Rogerson.

During the intervening period Ruxton's house had received a very thorough going-over and a large number of articles were removed and taken up to Edinburgh. One notable piece of evidence was a sheet taken from Mrs Ruxton's bed, which was examined and found to be identical in every way to the sheet wrapped round some of the body parts in the Linn, a peculiar selvedge being common to both. The police also noted on the wall of the sitting room a painting of Mrs Ruxton, commissioned from a local artist by the doctor.

In a triumph of medical detective work, Professors Glaister and Brash and their team had finally fitted together the bones and the remaining flesh, the estimated height of both bodies matching those of Isabella Ruxton and Mary Rogerson. It was noted that on 'Body No. 2' the ends of the fingers were missing and the left foot was mutilated, whereas in what remained of 'Body No. 1' much of the flesh had been cut from the head and the eyes had been removed, as had the two upper incisor teeth.

The trial began on Monday 2 March 1936. Extra rooms had to be prepared for the 115 witnesses who were due to give evidence and for more than 200 Crown exhibits. Appearing before Mr Justice Singleton for the Crown were Mr J.C. Jackson KC, Mr Maxwell Fyffe KC and Mr Hartley Shawcross, all three experienced men and veterans of many criminal trials. For the defence

The bath in which Ruxton cut up the bodies of his victims, now a horse trough. (Anthony Rae)

Close-up of the plaque by Ruxton's bath. (Anthony Rae)

were Norman Birkett KC and Phillip Kershaw KC, also a formidable team. The whole of the morning and into the afternoon were needed for the opening statement by the prosecution. Evidence was given as to the doctor's insane rages and his wife's sister, Mrs Nelson, caused a sensation when she gave evidence that she had seen Ruxton ill-treating his wife; letters from Ruxton to her were read out, begging her to help him get his wife back. These letters were written in early October and claimed that Isabella was trying to help Mary Rogerson, who was in 'a certain condition'. Former employees of the Ruxtons also gave evidence as to the doctor's treatment of his wife and in addition there was evidence of the differing stories that Ruxton had told to account for the absence of the two women.

The prosecution told the court that her sisters had last seen Isabella on 14 September at Blackpool. They had watched the illuminations and at around 11.30 p.m. Isabella had set off to drive back to Lancaster. She was never seen alive again, except by the prisoner. Mary Rogerson was last seen at around 7.30 p.m. on the same day by a Mrs Jackson, when she called at the house to pick up her children who had been attending a party there. The prosecution suggested that both women met their deaths on the landing at the top of the stairs outside Mary's bedroom, because there was evidence of a great amount of human blood which had flooded down the stairs and which all Ruxton's frantic efforts had not been able to remove. It was known that Mary Rogerson had a squint (both eyes had been removed from her skull) and that she had been vaccinated on the left upper arm, the marks being plainly present on Body No. 1. Isabella suffered from a bunion on her left foot and this portion of the body had been excised. She also had prominent teeth – and there were fourteen recent extractions in the skull of Body No. 2. Flexible casts of left feet from Body No. 1 and Body No. 2 fitted the shoes of Mary Rogerson and Isabella Ruxton precisely – little by little, the evidence was putting a rope around Ruxton's neck.

A tour de force was the photographic evidence, which was right at the cutting edge of the technology of the time. Taken from the murder house, a formal picture of Mrs Ruxton, in ball gown and tiara, was enlarged to life size and made into a transparency, which was then compared to similar life-sized transparencies of the two skulls. When offered up to the Ruxton picture, it was obvious that the skull of Body No. 1 did not match, but the transparency of Body No. 2 fitted exactly. The skull bones, the nasal cavity and the remaining teeth all matched and a composite picture was shown to the court, whereby Mrs Ruxton's features and her tiara were effectively superimposed over the picture of her skull. This was the first time that this technique had been used in a British court to catch a killer and was a considerable triumph for the technicians involved.

As the trial proceeded, it became obvious to everyone, including the accused, that the case against him had been proved several times over. A final nail in the

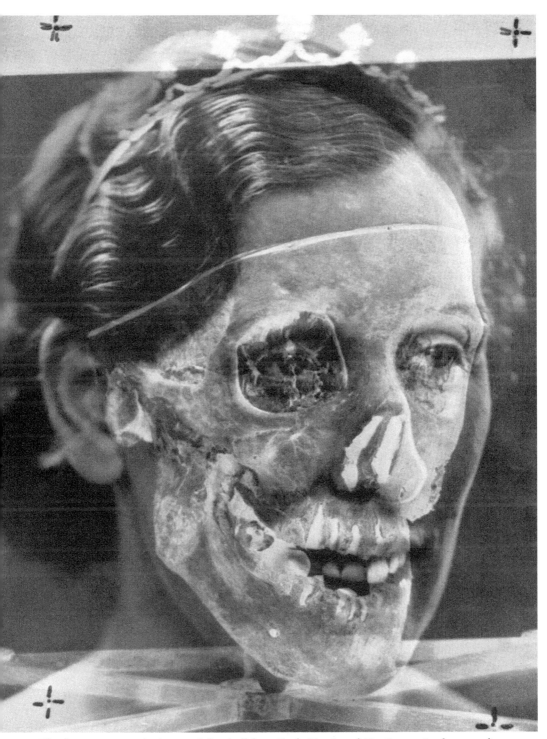

The famous composite image of the skull from Body No. 2 and Mrs Ruxton's photograph.
(Edinburgh University Forensic Department)

THIS IS THE LAST WILL AND TESTAMENT

of me

BUCK RUXTON of 2 Dalton Square Lancaster in the County of
Lancaster Registered Medical Practitioner 1. I Revoke all
wills heretofore made by me 2. I Appoint Charles Frederick
Gardner of Lancaster aforesaid Solicitor and The Public
Trustee to be the Executors and Trustees of this my will and
the Trustees or Trustee for the time being of my will are
herein referred to as my trustees 3. I Give Devise and
Bequeath all my estate and effects both real and personal
whatsoever and wheresoever and of what nature or kind soever
unto my trustees Upon Trust to sell my real estate and to
sell call in and convert into money such part of my personal
estate as shall not consist of money and to hold the net
proceeds of such sales calling in and conversion and the
ready money of which I may die possessed (hereinafter called
my trust estate) Upon trust thereout to pay all my just
debts and testamentary expenses and the sum of three guineas

the income accruing from the investments of my trust estate
in order to effect each year a certain minimum sum of money
requisite for the maintenance and education and all worldly
necessities of my said three children during the trust period
of twenty years so far as may be found to be feasible
I solemnly desire that my daughters should pursue studies
in Medicine and become qualified Registered Medical
Practitioners and my son should pursue a course of studies
in law with a view to either being enrolled as a Solicitor
or being called to the English Bar I solemnly desire this
my last wish to be carried out as far as is humanly possible
both by the strict supervision of my trustees over my children
and by the diligent application and industry of my children
themselves 4. In the event of any of my children dying under
the age of twenty one years the surviving child or children

Two extracts from the office copy of Buck Ruxton's will, leaving instructions that his daughters should pursue studies in medicine and his son become a lawyer, and bequeathing a non-existent estate. (Lancashire Public Record Office)

coffin was provided by the carpet and the bloodstained suit of clothes given by the doctor to Mrs Hampshire and which he had several times implored her to burn.

The only witness for the defence was Buck Ruxton himself and he could make no headway against the persistent questioning of the prosecution. He tried to convince the court that the bloodstains on the carpet were the result of a miscarriage suffered by his wife some months before; and when questioned about the suit he claimed that there were 'two or three years' accumulation of blood' on it, as he always wore it for the messy jobs like a confinement or a circumcision. The suggestion by Mr Jackson that no respectable doctor would ever wear a suit in that condition reduced him to incoherent rage.

Mr Justice Singleton summed up, reminding the jury that the prisoner must be given any benefit of the doubt and that it was not for him to prove his innocence but rather for the prosecution to show him guilty. The jury retired at 3.58 p.m. and returned just one hour and four minutes later to bring in a verdict of 'Guilty'. The judge donned the black cap and, telling the accused, 'You have been convicted on evidence that can leave no doubt upon the mind of anyone' [trial transcript], he sentenced Ruxton to hang.

Up and down the country petitions were raised for respite of the death sentence, as was usually the case after major murder trials, more out of sentiment than any belief that Ruxton was innocent. In Lancaster more than 6,000 people signed within the week. An appeal was heard on 27 April which, despite Birkett's best efforts, was disdainfully swept aside by Lord Hewart of Bury and his two fellow judges. So on the morning of 12 May 1936 a dense crowd gathered outside Strangeways Prison in Manchester and dispersed only when a prison officer placed on the heavy entrance doors the official certificate that confirmed the sentence had been carried out.

The News of the World published a 'confession', supposedly signed by Ruxton, which stated that he killed Isabella in a fit of temper because he thought that she had been with a man. Mary Rogerson had been present at the time and had to be killed as well.

In his will, written while he was awaiting trial, Ruxton asked his executor, the family solicitor Mr Gardner, to ensure that his three children received a good education and stipulated that his two daughters should study medicine and that his son should study law, with a view to becoming either a solicitor or a barrister. Norman Birkett was left a canteen of mother-of-pearl-handled silver fish knives and forks (which he refused to accept) and Mr Gardner was to have a leopard-skin rug and a polar bear rug – the latter was eventually rolled up and stored in the outside toilet at Gardner's office.

In the event the will was useless and the children were left penniless, as the net value of the estate, at £1,765 7s 10d, was insufficient to pay Ruxton's debts of more than £3,000, including the substantial costs of his defence.

M.4

In His Majesty's High Court of Justice.

The District Probate Registry at LANCASTER

BE IT KNOWN that *Buck Ruxton of 2 Dalton Square, Lancaster in the county of Lancaster*

died on the *12th* day of *May*, *1936* *at Manchester in the said county.*

AND BE IT FURTHER KNOWN that at the date hereunder written the last Will and Testament *with a codicil thereto*

(a copy whereof is hereunto annexed) of the said deceased was proved and registered in the District Probate Registry of His Majesty's High Court of Justice at LANCASTER and that Administration of all the Estate which by law devolves to and vests in the personal representative of the said deceased was granted by the aforesaid Court to *Charles Frederick Gardner of 31 Sun Street, Lancaster aforesaid Solicitor, one of the executors*

named in the said *Will — Power reserved to the other executor named in the said Will*

And it is hereby certified that an Affidavit for Inland Revenue has been delivered wherein it is shewn that the gross value of the said Estate in *Great Britain,* (exclusive of what the said deceased may have been possessed of or entitled to as a Trustee and not beneficially) amounts to *£1765 - 7 - 10. net value of personal estate — Nil*

Dated the *10th* day of *June*, *1936*

C. O. French

District Registrar.

M12812 4/34
JR Probate.

Extracted by *C. Fred Gardner, Solicitor, Lancaster*

Probate of the estate of Buck Ruxton, showing a value of £1,765 gross but nil net. (© Crown Copyright)

St Helen's Church, Overton, where Mary Rogerson was finally laid to rest in 1936.
(Author)

A life policy for £6,000 which he had been relying on, was voided, as the insurance company claimed that Ruxton was responsible for his own death. For many years after Ruxton was hanged the premises at 2 Dalton Square remained closed and empty, never again housing a family. In 1982 the house was taken over by Lancaster City Council and remains in their possession to this day. The bath in which Ruxton dismembered his unfortunate victims is now used as a horse trough at Lancashire Constabulary HQ.

For years after the crime, Lancashire children sang:

> Red stains on the carpet,
> Red stains on the knife,
> Oh Doctor Buck Ruxton,
> You murdered your wife.

7

ONE DEATH SENTENCE TOO MANY

Manchester, 1946

Walter Rowland was one of life's losers. Born in 1908 in the small Derbyshire town of New Mills, he left school at fourteen with little in the way of qualifications or prospects and started work as an engineering apprentice, but soon quit and joined the army, as much to get away from New Mills as anything else. Soon, finding the army as uncongenial as engineering, he begged his parents to buy him out.

After several menial jobs, he again joined the army but was discharged in quick time as being medically unfit; this setback was followed by another when on 30 June 1927 he was accused and found guilty of causing grievous bodily harm to Miss May Schofield by attempted strangulation – just after he had tried to commit suicide by hanging. A three-year term in Borstal was handed down, of which he served two, being released in 1929. He returned to a succession of labouring jobs, none of which lasted long, and in the meantime acquired several more convictions, including one for robbery.

His bad luck continued when his wife died in childbirth only ten months after their marriage in 1930. In September 1931 he married again, this time to Miss Annie May Schofield – presumably the girl he had tried to strangle in 1927. Miss Schofield was evidently a young lady who was either desperate or extremely forgiving, but unfortunately this marriage did not seem to end Rowland's run of ill fortune, as he continued his attempts to commit suicide, none of which was successful. (Attempted suicide was, of course, a crime punishable by imprisonment in those days.) The couple set up home at 2 Cheetham Hill Cottages, Mellor, a bleak, windswept collection of houses not far from New Mills, and in 1932 Annie May gave birth to a girl who was christened Mavis Agnes.

On 2 March 1934 Rowland was due to appear at the magistrate's court in Stockport after cheating a cab driver out of his fare of £3, but for some reason he did not attend the hearing, despite the fact that later in the day this non-appearance seemed to be a great worry to him. During the day, while her husband was out, Annie had gone through the pockets of a pair of his trousers – something that she evidently did on regular occasions – and had discovered one of her stockings stuffed inside. Puzzled, she put it back but said nothing.

When Rowland arrived home at around 4.30 p.m. he bought a newspaper and searched feverishly through it until he found a small paragraph saying that a warrant had been issued for his arrest for non-attendance at the hearing. He questioned his wife as to whether anybody had been asking for him – presumably meaning someone from the court – but she had seen no one. Rowland then suggested that it would be best if he went into hiding, but he had no money and made as if to break into the electricity meter – Annie May threatened that she would leave him if he did so. At just after 5.15 that evening she left the house to see relatives in New Mills, leaving her husband alone with their daughter, and at around 7 o'clock Rowland was seen running to the bus stop by the Devonshire Arms, where he boarded the bus for Stockport. At 7.45 Mrs Rowland returned to find the house in darkness, and on going upstairs she discovered her child in the cot, seemingly asleep. However, a closer look showed that the baby had a woman's stocking wound tightly round its throat and appeared to be dead.

Meanwhile, Walter Rowland had gone to a public house in Stockport where he picked up a woman and set off with her to go to New Brighton by taxi. There seems to have been no reason for this trip and it was after midnight when they arrived, only for Rowland to pretend that he did not know the address and to suggest that he should go to the local police station to make enquiries. He set off (followed by the taxi-driver, who suspected that Rowland was trying to dodge paying his fare) and walked into the police station, where he told a completely spurious and unnecessary story about having travelled to the town with three men and a woman who were all looking for lodgings. At that moment the taxi-driver, Mr Grimshaw, arrived and a row developed. Rowland and Grimshaw were taken into separate rooms and Rowland pulled from his pocket the newspaper he had bought earlier in the evening. Pointing to the paragraph which mentioned him, he said to Police Constable Wesley, 'Ring up the police at Mellor; they will tell you something more serious than that.' After enquiries were made he was taken to Wallasey police station, where he was charged with the murder of his daughter and put in the cells.

At the subsequent trial, as if his poor wife had not suffered enough, Rowland's defence was to accuse her of murdering their baby. When Rowland was found guilty and sentenced to death, she promptly left him and Mellor for ever. Surprisingly, the jury added a recommendation for mercy to their guilty verdict and, after an appeal failed, the death sentence was

commuted to life imprisonment, but he was released in 1942, having served
only eight years. This was a time when the country was at war; men were
needed and Rowland again went into the army. He was demobbed in June
1946 and returned to live with his parents in New Mills. War service had
done little for him and he again found it difficult to find employment. He
adopted a wandering sort of life, often being away from home for days at
a time, sending parcels of clothing back to New Mills for his long-suffering
mother to launder and post back to him wherever he happened to be. Four
months after demob he was spending much of his free time in low-grade pubs
and drinking houses, interspersed with overnight stays at dingy common
lodging houses, which had little to commend them apart from the fact that
they were cheap. Although Rowland later claimed in a statement to the police
to be 'proud of his body', he obviously did not object to subjecting it to beds
of doubtful cleanliness and to poor-quality food.

On the evening of Saturday 19 October 1946 a woman called Olive
Balchin had an appointment with a man whom she had known for about two
months. Olive was another down-and-out whose life had been affected by
the war, and with no proper home of her own she was living in a hostel run
by Manchester Corporation. She was about 40, of medium height, with dyed
hair and she scraped a meagre living as a prostitute, wandering the streets
of central Manchester looking for someone to buy her a meal and offering
herself afterwards for the price of a ten-shilling note. Her clients were almost
always in the same situation as herself, jobless and homeless, drifting from
place to place; the man she was waiting for on this particular evening had
become a sort of 'regular'.

Deansgate, one of the main thoroughfares in the city centre, had been
a street of handsome buildings before the war – built in the late Victorian
period to house upmarket shops, the prosperous merchants who traded at the
Corn Exchange and the lawyers, bankers and accountants who serviced their
community. It had suffered considerably during the bombing and was now
almost derelict, but the ordinary people of Manchester were built of stern
stuff and returned to their roots almost as soon as the bombs stopped falling.
One such was James Acarnley, of 89 Cumberland Street, who was taking his
dog for a walk on Sunday morning, 20 October 1946, when his attention was
attracted by two young boys who were pointing to something at the back of
a bombed-out building at the junction of Deansgate and Cumberland Street.
Before the bombing the building had boasted six tall, elegant windows on
either side of an imposing front portico, but it had taken a direct hit and now
only the skeleton of the ground floor façade remained, open to the sky.

At the rear of the building, in one corner amid a pile of rubble and dock
leaves, was the body of Olive Balchin, lying on her left side with her right
knee folded beneath her. Police photographs taken at the scene show that

Manchester's Deansgate as it was before the Blitz. (Author's collection)

she was wearing a skirt, stockings and a dark-coloured, calf-length overcoat with wide lapels and four large, white buttons at the front, with a similar button at each wrist. A beret-type hat lay nearby and she had been badly beaten about the head, the right side of the face being badly disfigured by deep indentations through one of which traces of brain were protruding. Mr Acarnley could see that the girl was dead and ran off to fetch the police, who soon arrived at the scene, led by Sergeant Thomas James Ross. They immediately started a search of the area and found, not far from the body, a hammer with a wooden shaft and a piece of paper in which the hammer appeared to have been wrapped. The body was taken to the Platt Lane mortuary, where it was identified by William Angood, who said that he had known the girl for about nine years, although he had not seen her for about three years. It is not clear how the police managed to find this man so quickly, although it is possible that Olive had his address on her when she died. The resident manageress of the corporation hostel told the police that the dead girl had stayed there for the past seven weeks and that the last time she had seen her was on 18 October.

The newspapers soon got hold of the story and the police arranged for a photograph of the hammer to have a prominent position in the Manchester *Evening News*. Almost immediately they received a call from Edward MacDonald, a licensed broker with a shop at 3 Downing Street, Ardwick, just over a mile away from the murder site; he told the police that he had purchased such a hammer on 19 October and had sold it almost immediately. The hammer was not one of the ordinary kind, but was a special one used by leather-dressers and as such it would not be of much use for general purposes. He had told the purchaser as much, but the man merely replied, 'It will suit my purpose', paid the 3s 6d asked, and left the shop, walking off in the direction of the city centre. Mr MacDonald was able to say that the hammer had several distinguishing marks, including a figure '4' stamped into the head and a wooden haft that was not the original one. He also gave a detailed description of the man who bought it as being of clean, respectable appearance, 28 to 32 years old, 5ft 7 or 8in in height, darkish hair, medium build, very pale face, thin features, clean shaven, and wearing a dark suit, white soft collar and shirt, dark tie and a dark fawn cotton raincoat. The customer had taken the hammer away wrapped in paper, which the shopkeeper had torn off a roll.

The post-mortem was conducted by Dr Charles Evans Jenkins, who described the dead woman as being aged between 40 and 50, which was a little older than her real age although the life she had been leading probably contributed to her appearance. She had received several blows to the head and face with a blunt instrument; the bone round the right eye was broken and there were other injuries. Shown the hammer that Sergeant Ross had found at the scene, he said that the injuries were consistent with having been caused by such an implement.

The police had little to go on at this stage and they commenced a routine trawl around the lodging houses and hostels of the area. A telephone call from Mr Norman Mercer, licensee of the Dog and Partridge, a local public house, revealed that late on 19 October he had locked up his establishment and had taken his dog for a walk along Deansgate before going to bed. A man and a woman were quarrelling near to the scene of the murder, although he could not say what the argument was about. The man was of medium build, with dark hair, and wore a dark suit, and Mercer particularly noticed that the girl was wearing a dark coat that featured large buttons. Mrs Elizabeth Copley, a waitress in the Queen's Café just off Deansgate, was interviewed by the police and told them that she had seen Olive Balchin, whom she knew, coming into the café with another woman on the evening of 19 October and that a man joined them soon afterwards. She, too, had noticed the large buttons on Olive's coat and was able to identify the coat from a police photograph. The man had his hair thickly plastered with grease and was carrying a small parcel wrapped in paper.

During the course of these enquiries, a complaint was made to the police that someone named Roland (*sic*) had borrowed a raincoat which he had not returned and that the man, who had a criminal record, was regularly in the Manchester area and was presently lodging at the Services' Transit dormitory. When the police arrived at the hostel they found Rowland asleep in bed, quickly woke him and told him to get dressed and come with them to police headquarters. 'Is it about that coat?' asked the hardly conscious Rowland and then, 'You don't want me for the murder of that effing woman do you?' – a phrase that he later denied saying.

At the police station, Rowland was questioned by Inspector Stainton and agreed that he had known the dead girl for about two months and had had intercourse with her on two occasions, once on a bomb site and once in a doorway; but he insisted that the bomb site was not the one in Deansgate where the body had been found. He said that he had seen Olive in a café on 18 October, when they had something to eat and he had arranged to see her again the following evening, although he had no intention of doing so and in fact did not see her. He also told the police that he thought Olive had given him VD and that if he could be sure of this, he would have strangled her. (The post-mortem showed that Olive Balchin was free from infection.) During questioning Rowland said, 'I am admitting nothing, for it's only a fool's game to do that. I can account for where I was. I was at home at New Mills when she was murdered. I didn't come back to Manchester that night.' Later he changed his story and told the police, 'I did come back to Manchester. I got a lift in a car and then went to a pub for a drink. I didn't go into Deansgate. I stayed in the Ardwick district, where I had supper and stayed at Grafton House, 67 Hyde Road. I didn't get in until after one o'clock.' After further questioning Rowland changed his story yet again and claimed that he had stayed at 36 Hyde Road. On Sunday afternoon, 27 October, Rowland was put on an identification parade, where Mrs Copley, Mr MacDonald and Mr Mercer all identified him. MacDonald and Mercer had no doubts, going straight to Rowland, whereas Mrs Copley showed some hesitation and walked up and down the line several times before putting her hand on Rowland's shoulder, saying, 'I'm not certain, but I think this is the man.'

The police now considered that they had a good enough case against Rowland and the trial commenced at the Manchester Autumn Assizes on 12 December before Mr Justice Sellers. Basil Nield KC and Mr Basil Wingate-Saul appeared for the Crown and Kenneth Burke and Mr H. Openshaw for the accused. After evidence of identification and the post-mortem report, Edward MacDonald was called into the witness box, where he described the sale of the hammer and identified the man in the dock as the person who bought it. Referring back to the preliminary hearing at the police court, defence counsel suggested that he had not been able to identify Rowland as

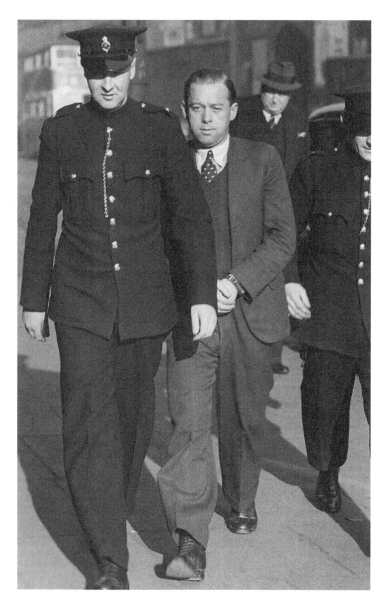

Walter Rowland under arrest. Note the slicked-down hair, appearing quite dark. (popperfoto. com)

being in the courtroom on that occasion, to which MacDonald replied, 'Yes sir. I was a bit flustered. He had his head bent on the table.' Pressed to have another look round, he had asked for Rowland to stand up and this time had identified him straight away.

Much was made of the colour of Rowland's hair, stated by MacDonald and Mrs Copley to be 'dark', whereas it was obvious to all in the courtroom that the accused's hair was light brown. Both witnesses said that Rowland was wearing a considerable amount of hair dressing which had the effect of darkening it, although when his mother was called to give evidence she stated that her son never wore anything on his hair and had, in fact, given a bottle of brilliantine away the previous year as he did not use it. A press photograph taken of Rowland on his way to the police station, under arrest, shows quite clearly that he was indeed in the habit of wearing hair dressing and that this application did tend to give an appearance of dark hair.

Rowland's statement was then read out to the court, and included the following:

> I first met Olive Balchin near Victoria Station about seven or eight weeks ago. Since then, I've met her on three or four occasions. I have had intercourse with her twice, once on Baxendale's blitzed building site and the other time in a doorway in a side street. Shortly after I had intercourse with her, I suspected that I had contracted venereal disease . . . . On Friday night, 18 October, I went to Littlewoods Café in Piccadilly and I saw Olive Balchin there. I bought her cakes and tea. It was in my mind to find out whether she had this complaint without letting her know. I left her at about quarter past nine and went for a drink in the Feathers. Later I went to the NAAFI and stayed there. . . . On 19 October I knocked about town and went to the post office for a parcel I was expecting [the laundry done for him by his mother], but it wasn't there so I decided to go home for it. I got a bus to New Mills and arrived there at about quarter past eight. I went to my mother's house, changed my things there and put on all clean stuff. Then I came back on the bus to Stockport, arriving at about ten o'clock. I had a few drinks in the bottom Wellington.* I took a bus to Manchester and got off at Ardwick and had some supper in a chip shop. I made a few enquiries as to where I could get bed and breakfast and was directed to Hyde Road. I went there and stayed at no. 36. It would be about half past midnight or quarter to one. I booked in and signed the register. I only stayed one night. I have given the black shoes I was wearing in Littlewoods on the Friday to a man for the price of a packet of fags. The raincoat I was wearing on the Friday, I borrowed. I have given it back to an American known to all the boys by the nickname of 'Slim'.

Dr J.B. Firth, Director of the Home Office Laboratory at Preston, gave evidence that there was a bloodstain on Rowland's left shoe, which he identified as human blood, but he could not ascertain the blood group. There

---

* The Wellington public house is built against a steep slope and it was possible to walk in at the upper street level (known as the 'Top Wellington') and after going down a flight of stairs, emerge into the bar some 60ft below ('Bottom Wellington').

The 'Top' and 'Bottom' Wellingtons, the public house visited by Rowland on the night of the murder and where he claimed to have seen two policemen. (popperfoto.com)

were no other bloodstains on Rowland's clothes, but in his trouser turn-ups was a quantity of debris, including fragments of brick dust, cement, charcoal, clinker and withered leaf tissue, identical to a sample from the murder scene. There were also two hairs that matched samples taken from Olive Balchin's head.

In his own defence, Rowland insisted that he had never used grease as a dressing for his hair and admitted that there was every likelihood that he had contracted VD while in the forces. He described his journey to and from New Mills on the night of the murder, and a major point of his evidence concerning the Wellington public house was that he had seen two police officers leaving it at around 10.30. Evidence was given that two officers were in the Wellington at around that time; Police Sergeant Jones stated that it was an incidental part of his duty to visit licensed premises in the town and that he had been in the pub on other occasions at about closing time. Rowland said that he had never been in MacDonald's shop and that he did not see Olive Balchin on 19 October. He now claimed to have arrived in Manchester and to have spent the night at 81 Brunswick Street (another change from his original statement), where he signed the visitors' book and left at around 10 a.m. on the Sunday. The visitors' book was produced showing that he had signed in on the 19th, but that was also the date shown for his departure. This was obviously an error and the proprietor, Mr Frank Beaumont, confirmed that the arrival date was correct, Rowland having arrived at about 11.15 p.m., and that he had left on Sunday, the 20th. It was possible, Beaumont said, that Rowland could have gone out again on the night of the 19th and returned later without his knowledge.

The defence submissions ended on Saturday 14 December, and Rowland was left waiting until the following Monday for the closing speeches to be made and the jury to retire. It took just under two hours for them to return with a unanimous verdict of 'Guilty', to which Rowland replied, 'May God forgive you. You have condemned an innocent man.' In accordance with usual practice, the Clerk of the Assize asked Rowland if he had anything to say as to why sentence of death should not be passed according to law. Rowland then made the following remarkable speech:

> Yes I have, my Lord. I have never been a religious man, but as I have sat in this Court during these last few hours the teachings of my boyhood have come back to me, and I say in all sincerity and before you and this Court that when I stand in the Court of Courts before the Judge of Judges I shall be acquitted of this crime. The killing of this woman was a terrible crime, but there is a worse crime been committed now, my Lord, because someone with a knowledge of this crime is seeing me sentenced today for a crime which I did not commit. I have a firm belief that one day it will be proved in God's own time that I am totally innocent of this charge, and the day will come when this case will be quoted in the Courts of this country to show what can happen to a man in a case of mistaken identity. I am going to face what lies before me with the fortitude and calm that only a clear conscience can give. That is all I have got to say, my Lord.

It was not unusual in the days of the death penalty for such orations, containing flowery language and appeals to the Almighty, to be delivered from the dock by those who might well not have seen the inside of a church since their christening. The judge, having heard many similar protestations in the past, wasted no time and sentenced Rowland to death. What no one in the court knew – least of all the accused – was that there would be a startling development within days, and that Rowland's protestation of mistaken identity would shortly trouble the minds of some of the highest authorities in the land.

On 24 January 1947 a prisoner in Liverpool's Walton jail, David John Ware, made a statement to Detective Inspector Stainton concerning the Rowland case, having confessed in a short statement to the governor of the prison two days earlier. Ware was a petty criminal who resembled Rowland only vaguely, in that he was also of medium height and slim build, wore his hair neatly brushed back and was also in the habit of dressing in a suit. The statement said that Ware stole some money from a Salvation Army hostel on 18 October 1946 and travelled to Manchester, where he stayed the night with a girl. On the Saturday he wandered around the city centre trying to get up a scheme to obtain money and, in his own words, 'I decided in the afternoon to buy a hammer for purpose of committing robbery with violence.' He bought a hammer near the railway station, and at 6 p.m. he met Olive Balchin and suggested going to the pictures with her, the idea being to kill time till it got dark. They came out of the cinema around 9 o'clock and caught a bus to the city centre, where they eventually ended up at the Deansgate bomb site. During attempted intercourse, Ware felt the girl going through his pockets and suggested that they should move further back into the ruins, where no one would see them. He then attacked her with the hammer and left her for dead, first travelling to Stockport and on the Sunday walking to Buxton and then on to Chapel-en-le-Frith, where he stayed the night at an institution. On the Monday he hitch-hiked to Sheffield and surrendered to the police for the Salvation Army robbery.

Ware followed this up in a statement to Rowland's solicitor in which he expanded the details, including the fact that he paid 3s 6d for the hammer and that it was wrapped up in paper. He described Olive Balchin as wearing a light-brown, tam-o'-shanter-type hat and a dark coat, the buttons on which appeared to Ware to be unsuitable. He repeated his claim that Balchin had robbed him of a ten-shilling note, but appeared vague as to what happened next, up until the time he surrendered to the police. He admitted that he had read the newspapers, which gave full details of the finding of Olive Balchin's body, but claimed that he had not read anything about the police court proceedings or of Rowland's trial. The first he had heard about Rowland's conviction and sentence was on Saturday 18 January, when a fellow prisoner at Walton told him about it.

In the meantime, Rowland's application to the Court of Criminal Appeal had been postponed for fourteen days and was eventually heard on 10 February, when an attempt was made to call Ware to give evidence. This request was turned down by the Appeal Court judges, on the basis that if Ware were allowed to give evidence, the court would have to come to some conclusion as to his guilt or otherwise and would therefore have been usurping the function of a jury. They did, however, allow the calling of two further witnesses, Walter Haydn Ellwood, the manager of the Plaza Cinema, Stockport and Henry Somerville, who both gave evidence as to the film being shown on 19 October. Somerville also supported Rowland's presence in the Wellington around 10.30 on the same evening, and other details which were of little relevance. The judges considered that this new evidence would not have affected the minds of the jury and after remarking that the Home Secretary, with his much wider powers, could if he so wished order an inquiry, the appeal was dismissed.

Three days later Mr J.C. Jolley QC was appointed to conduct such an inquiry, during the course of which Ware made a third statement, on 22 February, in which he withdrew his first two confessions. This time he claimed that both previous statements were untrue and that he did not know Olive Balchin at all, neither had he had any hand in her death. He had made the original statements out of 'swank', because he wanted to be a 'hero'. During his stay in Walton jail awaiting trial, from 23 October 1946 to 15 January 1947, he had, as an unconvicted prisoner, access to the daily newspapers and had read all about the murder in the *Daily Herald* and other publications, also discussing it with fellow prisoners. He now gave a detailed explanation as to his movements on 19 October, in which there was no mention of Olive Balchin whatsoever, and his statement concluded with the words, 'I would like to say that I am sorry I have given the trouble I have and I didn't realise the serious consequences it might entail had the confession been believed.'

Mr Jolley concluded his inquiry on 25 February. He knew about the contradictory statements made by Ware, having being present when Ware retracted his confession, and he had also attended an identity parade when Ware was put up and seen by Mr MacDonald, Mr Mercer and Mrs Copley – all of whom stated definitely that there was no one in the line that they recognised. In his opinion, all the details in Ware's three statements could have been gained from newspaper reports, statements inserted at the instance of the police, discussions with prisoners and from his own imagination. Discrepancies as to which lodging house Ware had used on 19 October, and evidence from Dr J.B. Firth that he had found no blood on Ware's person or his clothes and that the detritus in his trouser turn-ups did not match that found at the death scene, added to Mr Jolley's certainty that Ware had had nothing to do with the death of Olive Balchin. Ware had also indicated in his first two statements that he had killed Balchin at around 10 p.m.; but a witness, Wilfred Gosling, told Mr Jolley that he had been walking his dog in Deansgate at about 10.30 p.m. on 19 October, and the dog, being a particularly fierce one, would have refused to leave the scene if it had smelt blood.

The closing parts of the report referred to Ware's mental state, including the fact that he had spent three weeks in the Buckinghamshire Mental Hospital in July 1941 and that he was discharged from the army in July 1943 on the grounds of manic depressive psychosis. The final point was that there was nothing in Ware's appearance that might have led to his being taken for Rowland (this impression being shared by Superintendent Barratt, who had assisted with the report). Jolley was satisfied that there were no grounds for thinking there had been any miscarriage of justice in Rowland's conviction. The accused man was hanged by Albert Pierrepoint on 27 February 1947 at Strangeways Prison, less than a mile from the scene of the crime.

Four years later, on 10 July 1951, David John Ware attempted to kill a woman using a hammer which he had bought only that day. He was tried for attempted murder, found guilty but insane and committed to Broadmoor, where he committed suicide by hanging himself on 1 April 1954. News of the attempted murder caused a certain amount of disquiet at the time. However, despite Rowland's impassioned statement from the dock, his final letter to his parents – in which he reiterated his innocence and wrote, 'I tell you mother and dad that before my maker I swear I am completely innocent of the death of that poor woman' – and the muddying of the waters by Ware's confessions, it seems certain that Ware was following a long line of inadequates who routinely involve themselves with notorious cases, having taken the trouble to familiarise themselves with all the details. The police are well used to numbers of people coming in to confess to murders which hit the headlines, and it is for this reason that these days they always try to keep something back from the press, so that they can test the supposed murderer with information that only the real killer could have known.

One's mind is drawn to the case of James Hanratty, convicted and hanged for the murder of John Gregsten in a lay-by on the A6 near Slough in 1961. A man named Peter Alphon, who had been involved on the periphery of the case, having stayed in the same hotel as Hanratty just before the murder, regularly called press conferences for a number of years afterwards to confess to the crime, adopting known features of Hanratty's speech patterns that had been given in evidence at the trial. Alphon attracted considerable attention, but the police showed little interest in his ramblings, although Hanratty's family spent years trying to prove that their boy was innocent. In the public interest, Hanratty's body was recently exhumed and modern DNA testing, which was not available at the time of the trial, has proved 'incontrovertibly' – in the words of the Appeal Court judge – that he was guilty. Hanratty had, like Rowland, protested his innocence up till the last.

8

FOURTH TIME UNLUCKY

Southport, 1947

It was late spring of 1947 in the Lancashire seaside resort of Southport and the town was beginning to come back to life after the hardships of war. Two of its largest hotels had just been de-requisitioned by the War Ministry and although a power crisis in February had set Southport back a bit, the inhabitants were looking forward to welcoming their summer visitors and relieving them of their hard-earned holiday money. Labour was still in short supply and there was an unsatisfied demand for female domestic workers in the hotels, institutions and private houses, but the town council thought that this would probably sort itself out as the season wore on.

Southport was proud of its genteel ambience: the wide, colourful gardens that divided the beach from the promenade and the expensive shops on Lord Street, fronted by graceful colonnades of wrought iron and glass. Admittedly, the residents had to undergo a certain amount of ribbing from summer visitors, who joked about the absence of the sea – many of them complaining that Southport was now an inland resort and that the tide always seemed too far away – but at least, even if the location was not ideal for sea bathing, the children loved the wide expanses of golden sand. For those who insisted on a glimpse of the sea there was a choice between walking to the end of the pier, with its amusement arcade and tearoom, and riding there on the ever-popular narrow-gauge railway. The town was noted for its retirement and nursing homes, many of them large and expensive establishments situated along the promenade, intermingled with private houses, superior flats and hotels occupied for the most part by the professional classes and the well-to-do. The social scene, perforce in abeyance during the war, was now dusting down its glad rags and once again beginning to fill the columns of the local paper, the *Southport Visiter*.

Among the socialites flexing their wings at the time were the 66-year-old

View of the Promenade, Southport, 1930. The block where Dr Clements had his flat is two to the left from the smaller white building with the spire showing above it. (Author's collection)

Dr Robert George Clements and his wife Amy Victoria, or 'Vee' as he habitually called her. She was some nineteen years younger than her husband and the daughter of a widowed Lancashire industrialist who had died six months before the marriage leaving in excess of £20,000, a considerable sum in those days. They lived in an imposing flat at 20 The Promenade, one of the best addresses in Southport, although few of their friends had ever seen the inside of it. Paunchy and balding, the dapper Dr Clements was often to be seen with his wife at the productions of the Dramatic Society and the Southport Literary Society; he was also a member of the Film Society and of the Hospital Aid Society, and was a prominent freemason. His wife did not have the same brash, outgoing personality as her husband, but she busied herself doing good works, including serving on the committee of the International Women's Day, and she regularly attended Christ Church.

Clements, born in Ireland in 1882, had completed his medical studies in Edinburgh, becoming a Fellow of the Royal College of Surgeons in 1912. He also held the Diploma of Public Health from Belfast and was a Fellow of the Faculty of Insurance, contributing to the pages of *The Lancet* and the *British*

Medical Journal from time to time. Until the previous year he had been Deputy Medical Officer of Health at Blackburn, a post that he had taken up when some of the younger members of staff were called up for war service. He was now semi-retired, although he continued to attend a select number of private patients and his picture was regularly to be seen in the pages of the *Southport Visiter* at one social function or another.

Social gadabouts the doctor and his wife might have been, but they did little or no entertaining at home. Clements used to boast that he had never eaten a cooked meal in the flat, and let it be known that he and Vee preferred to eat out in restaurants. This was not unusual for people of their substantial means and it attracted little comment, although their many acquaintances might well have been shocked had they known that the good doctor and his wife lived in considerable squalor in their fashionable Promenade flat, with evidence of neglect and decay all around them. The couple were, to say the least, a little peculiar in their ways; but while Dr Clements might well have been lucky in his career, from which it was rumoured that he had amassed a sizeable fortune, he certainly appeared to have been unlucky in love. Victoria was, in fact, his fourth wife, the marriage having taken place in June 1940 at St George's Church, Hanover Square, London.

Clements's first wife was Edyth Anna Mercier, whom he married in Belfast in 1912, a wedding that was one of the high spots of the social season. Edyth was the daughter of a wealthy miller, ten years older than her husband, and she died in 1920 of a somewhat unusual ailment: sleeping sickness, the death certificate being signed by her husband. Her estate, according to the court records, had unaccountably dwindled to just £109 and, as she had not made a will, Letters of Administration were granted to her husband. Wife number two was another heiress, Mary McCleery, whom he married in Manchester in 1921. She died four years later aged 27, Letters of Administration having again been granted to the doctor, this time in the sum of £425. The death certificate signed by the grieving Dr Clements showed the cause of death as malignant endocarditis – inflammation of the lining membrane of the heart. 'Mary's death had been expected,' the doctor confided to family friends.

While Clements did not seem to the casual observer to be a particularly attractive catch in the matrimonial stakes, it was perhaps his social position and his rumoured wealth that attracted the ladies, for within three years he had married again – this time Sarah Kathleen Burke, known as Kathleen. She survived until 1939, dying of stomach cancer in the fashionable Southport Kenworthy Hydro, where her husband was by then the senior medical officer. The cremation certificate was signed by Dr Clements and another local doctor; for the third time there was no will, Clements once more taking out the Grant of Administration. Kathleen left just over £489, a modest sum, but while she might not have had all that much money she did have friends, one

The site of Kenworthy Hydro, where Clements's third wife died and where he was Medical Officer.
(Author)

218.	Twenty third May 1939 Kenworthys Hydro W.D.	Sarah Kathleen Clements	female	50 years	Wife of Robert George Clements M.D.
	a) myocarditis (b) malignant Pancreatitis Certified by E. A. Wilson M.B. to 16	R. G. Clements Widower of deceased In attendance Kenworthys Hydro Bath Street Southport		Twenty fourth may 1939	H. Barr. Registrar

*The death certificate of Sarah Kathleen Clements, third wife of Dr Clements. The cause of death was
certified as myocarditis and malignant pancreatitis by Dr Clements.* (© Crown Copyright)

of whom was Dr Irene Gayus. She was naturally upset at the death of her long-standing friend, especially as she had always considered Kathleen to be a lively and energetic person. She was also somewhat surprised to find that Kathleen had succumbed so quickly to cancer. In addition, her suspicions were aroused by the fact that she had seen Kathleen eat a hearty meal only two days before her death, something that would have been most unlikely if she was indeed suffering from stomach cancer. The doctor's action in signing his own wife's death certificate, while not illegal, was somewhat unethical and there were rumours that Clements had predicted his wife's demise almost to the day.

Dr Gayus decided to have a word about her suspicions with the Chief Constable of the Southport force, Major Michael Egan. She insisted that the funeral was imminent and there was no time to lose: in her opinion a post-mortem had to be carried out immediately. Unfortunately, by the time the police telephoned the mortuary to suspend the funeral arrangements it was too late; the body was already in the crematorium. It seems highly probable that Dr Clements knew nothing at all about this intervention, although if he had it might have saved another two, if not three, lives.

In 1947 the fourth wife, Amy, fell ill, due – so Clements said – to myeloid leukaemia, a malignant cancer of the blood. He kept a careful diary, describing in some detail the slow decline of his wife and claimed that on 26 May, the day before she died, the couple had gone for a short walk, during which Amy collapsed and had to be assisted home and put to bed. Two

The site of Astley Bank Nursing Home, where the last Mrs Clements died. (Author)

THE
SOUTHPORT VISITER

Ormskirk Herald   Formby Herald

1   Established 1844   SATURDAY MAY 31 1947   PUBLISHED ON TUESDAY THURSDAY & SATURDAY

E INQUEST OPENS TO-DAY

A OF DOCTOR AND WIFE

Stopped as
rs Assembled

:T GEORGE CLEMENTS, WELL-KNOWN
CTOR, WAS BEING RUSHED TO THE
,RY WHERE HE DIED WITHIN A FEW
MISSION YESTERDAY MORNING,
UNERAL SERVICE AT CHRIST CHURCH
MY VICTORIA CLEMENTS, WHO DIED
LE INFORMED THAT THE POLICE HAD
:LLATION OF THE INTERMENT.

't a note which is in the hands of the South-
ied and apparently asleep by a representative
nsible for his wife's funeral arrangements.
ir. Clements and informed the police.

and Mrs. | " Devoted Couple "
is fourth | Another friend said: " He and his
.e flat at | wife were devoted, in fact, I don't
Dr. and | know of a more devoted couple in
nediately | Southport."
       | During the past few months Dr. and

Dr. and Mrs. R. G. CLEMENTS.

Town to Exten

SOUTHPORT
"BITES

New Areas In E
Proposal:

SOUTHPORT'S boundary will reach to th
amended proposals obtain the approva
mission. These amended plans, decided u
Corporation Boundary Commission Committ
for the inclusion within the county boroug
Meols, Scarisbrick, Halsall, Downholland a
of Aughton and Altcar.

When originally announced, the town's
the borough boundaries to include Formb
Halsall and Downholland, and North Meols
including Banks. It will be seen that the
" bites " at two additional areas, as well
other areas it was first suggested should be

" Rates Would Jump "

The proposals will come before the | " Comm
Town Council next week. Meanwhile

The front page of the Southport Visiter, *31 May 1947, showing Dr Clements and his fourth wife.* (Southport Visiter)

doctors were sent for, the first to arrive being Dr Andrew Brown, followed by Dr John Holmes. Amy, having lost consciousness, was transferred to the Astley Bank Nursing Home, dying there at 9.15 a.m. the following day. Clements made another note in his diary: 'Adorable wife. She was good and devoted, never fair to herself.' Unusually, Dr Clements insisted that there should be a post-mortem on his fourth wife, and this was carried out privately on 28 May by 39-year-old Dr James Montague Houston, a somewhat shy young man who had started work as a pathologist at the Southport Infirmary just five months earlier at a salary of £1,250 per annum. Throughout the war he had served at Catterick Camp as pathologist, with the rank of major, and had become the senior surgeon responsible for 8,000 troops. He had a wife and two young boys, and only two weeks earlier he and his family had moved into a house of their own after a spell in rather cramped lodgings.

The post-mortem took nearly four hours and it is a curiosity of this case that it was conducted at the nursing home, a most unsuitable location for such a procedure to take place. The matron of the home was to say later that she would not have allowed the post-mortem to be carried out there had she known that it was to be a full examination, and not just an inspection of the brain. Dr Houston then took certain organs to Southport Infirmary for further examination and gave his opinion that Mrs Clements had died from myeloid leukaemia, as her husband had stated. Houston, junior doctor though he was, must have been fully aware that before he started his post-mortem he should have sought the consent of the local coroner, Mr Bolton. He would also have known that his action after the examination in instructing a laboratory technician to dispose of the specimens taken, including heart, brain and stomach contents, was out of order. The organs would normally have been returned to the body for burial or cremation as required. But then matters moved in an altogether unexpected direction.

When Amy had been examined before being admitted to the nursing home, Drs Brown and Holmes had both noticed that the pupils of her eyes were contracted to the size of pinpoints, often the sign of a morphine overdose. Once they had seen the certificate issued by Dr Houston, showing leukaemia as the cause of death, they went straight to the coroner with their suspicions. Dr Brown also visited Dr Houston and told him that he and his colleague strongly suspected that Amy had been poisoned with morphine administered by her husband. 'I wish to God I had known about that earlier', was the young doctor's reply. The coroner decided that he would have a word with the Chief Constable, Lt Col Harold Mighall, to discuss the way forward. After all, Dr Clements was a medical man with some stature in the town and if any suggestion came out that he had caused the death of his wife by morphine injection, there would be a scandal of enormous proportions. He was also aware that the police had had their suspicions about Dr Clements since the death of his third wife.

Mighall had been in his post for only about a year and was eager that this delicate situation should be handled with care. Amy's funeral was scheduled for Friday 30 May at Christ Church, which left no time to lose, and so Mighall immediately set off to visit Dr Clements. Affecting a jovial mood that ill became a man who had just lost his wife, Clements invited Mighall into the flat, which the policeman – to his surprise – found filthy and smelling of rotting food. 'Mrs Clements was unwell for some time and had not been able to keep the flat as clean as she would have wished,' explained Clements: but this worried Mighall even more. The couple were wealthy and could easily have afforded the services of a maid or cleaner to dispose of the empty milk bottles littering the floor, mixed up with table scraps, half-eaten tins of food, newspapers and empty pill boxes. By the side of the fireplace was a rotting grapefruit and a box of potatoes that had started to sprout – altogether a most surprising state of affairs for such a prominent professional man. 'Sorry about the state of the place,' Clements apologised for a second time. 'It's just that with everything . . .' his voice trailed off.

Plainly, Mighall was in no mood for small talk. 'I am interested in your wife's death,' he said bluntly. Clements appeared unperturbed. 'There is no cure for myeloid leukaemia,' he replied easily. 'Dr Houston was quite correct in his findings.' Leaving the matter there for the moment, Mighall was glad to get out into the fresh air and decided to visit Dr Houston, who seemed puzzled as to why the policeman was there. 'What exactly is the matter?' he asked. Mighall, determined not to give too much away, merely replied, 'Just routine, Dr Houston. One or two things about Mrs Clements's death are bothering us and in the first instance, I would like to know if you are certain that she died from natural causes?' Houston flushed. 'I made a thorough examination and ascertained the cause of death. What could possibly be wrong with that?' Mighall, sensing the man's nervousness, continued: 'When you were carrying out the post-mortem, did you think to search for drugs?' Houston looked even more worried. 'Certainly not. I have already said that I found the cause of death, so there was no need to look for anything else.' Houston confirmed that he had not used the nursing home's mortuary to carry out the post-mortem, but had used the patient's bed. This surprised the Chief Constable – a considerable amount of blood would have flowed during the examination – but in view of Houston's youth he put it down to the doctor's comparative inexperience in such matters. 'Can you tell me what you would think if you saw a patient with pinpoint pupils?' Mighall asked. 'That usually indicates morphine poisoning,' was the reply. 'Will there be another post-mortem?' Making a non-committal reply, Mighall left Dr Houston to his thoughts and realised that he was now in possession of several pieces of information about Clements that all tended to support a case of murder against him.

Miss Mary McKeefe, a servant in the next flat, informed the police that Mrs Clements had told her of occasional 'funny turns' that caused her to lose her voice and lapse into unconsciousness. 'The last attack,' Miss O'Keefe said, 'was about three weeks ago.' Another neighbour, Mrs Jean MacLachlan, said that she had seen Dr Clements and his wife return to the house at about 10.15 on the evening before she died, walking arm in arm and seemingly in good health and spirits. Yet another of Amy's friends, Mrs Ursula Clarenden, reported that for the past few months Dr Clements had refused her admission to the flat when she called to enquire after her friend, telling her that his wife needed rest and was not to be disturbed. The doctor had also taken the extreme step of having the telephone taken out, thus preventing Mrs Clarenden or anyone else from making contact with his wife that way; the whole affair, she thought, was very disturbing.

Mighall quietly made arrangements for a second post-mortem to be done on Amy Clements, this time by Dr W.H. Grace, a distinguished Home Office

pathologist, and the equally eminent Dr J.B. Firth, Director of the North
Western Forensic Laboratory. Dr Clements was asked if he would cooperate
by making an official identification of his wife's body and his diary entry for
29 May noted: 'Police contacted me and came and brought me to identify Vee
at the morgue for inquest tomorrow morning. *What is it all about?*'

Events then moved quickly. On the morning of 30 May, the people
gathering for the funeral of Amy Clements were surprised and shocked when
police arrived to call it off until further notice. Scandalised whispers were
exchanged as the mourners stood about in groups outside the church, puzzled
as to why the funeral of their friend and the wife of a respected medical man
of the town should have been halted in this fashion. Their questions would
intensify dramatically the next day, when the headline on the front page
of the *Visiter* screamed, 'Drama of Doctor and Wife – Funeral stopped as
Mourners Assembled.'

On the evening before the ceremony, a representative of the funeral directors
had called at 20 The Promenade to make final arrangements with Clements
and had found him in bed, unconscious. He was unable to rouse the doctor
and called the police. Dr Clements was taken to Southport Infirmary, where
he died a few minutes after admission. A note left by the dead man, addressed
to 'Ernest and George' (his only son and his brother), said, 'To whom it may
concern. I can no longer tolerate the diabolical insults to which I have recently
been exposed.' Now that Dr Clements was beyond the control of any earthly
agency, there was little point in delaying Amy's funeral any longer and it was
allowed to take place at Birkdale cemetery on 31 May. The *Southport Visiter*
noted a considerable number of wreaths, including those from 'Southport
Zionist and Literary Society', 'Vicar and Mrs Pickering (Christ Church)',
'Society and Friends of Czechoslovakia' and one simply marked 'Husband'.

The result of the second post-mortem on Amy Clements was not yet known
and the one on her husband had yet to take place, so the public were still very
much in the dark. To friends of the family it seemed to be just another in a

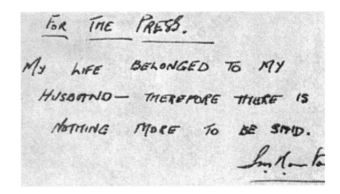

The Southport Visiter *showing a letter
written to the press by Mrs Houston after
her husband's suicide.* (Southport Visiter)

HPORT VISITER   THURSDAY   JUNE   26   1947

CLEMENTS' INQUEST—CONTINUED FROM PAGE ONE

e Tells How He Found Dying

Tablets
ι Flat

l it appear to you that Dr.
ston's conclusions at the examin-
; were definite? Did he appear
ave any doubt about the result?

continued his investigation into
other organs after he went back
ιe Infirmary?—Yes.

Result of Tests

he had then come to any con-
on other than the one he had
ed at, namely myeloid leukaemia.
ould have informed Dr. Holmes?
s.

I he ever tell you he suspected
other cause of death?—He did not
ne he suspected anything.

ery test you had applied resulted
ιe same conclusion—leukaemia?—
exoept the dilution test. All the
r tests—the films—pointed to con-
ation of Dr. Houston's opinion.

your experience do you usually
n the organs or have known
ι to be destroyed?—I don't know

DR. J. M. HOUSTON   MRS. CLEMENTS   DR. R. G. CLEMENTS

Mr. Carr: Is leukaemia a condition
which might arise suddenly?—Very
insidiously and sometimes very
suddenly.

So that although it may not appear
according to the blood count in
January, it might well appear in
May?—It might, but not, in this case,
sufficient to have caused death.

Mr. Carr: I am representing the son
of Dr. Clements, and it is for me if
I can to show that there is no cause
for any stigma to be attached to his
name. I say the pin-pointing of the
pupils of the eyes is not necessarily a
conclusive symptom of morphine
poisoning.

Mr. Mace's Questions

body of Mrs. Clements received by
him. He said that a kidney weighing
147 grams contained 164 milligrams
of morphine, approximately one
fiftieth of a grain of morphine.

The half spinal cord weighed 12
grams and a quantitative estimation
indicated that six grams of the spinal
chord contained .8 milligrams, or
approximately one fortieth of a grain
of morphine.

Dr. Firth said the material
submitted to him for examination was
limited and minus certain organs.

ARTICLES REMOVED FROM FLAT

Tubes of Tablets

Reporting on material recovered
from the Clements' flat, Dr. Firth said
these included a hypodermic syringe
which had no significance, but there
was a loose glass syringe, the plunger
of which was missing, and the inside
contained a crystallised deposit on
the side of the tube containing a
marked amount of morphine.

Since making his examination he
had again visited the flat and found
the plunger belonging to the syringe
under a small table about six feet
from the position where the body of
the syringe had been found, and
about four feet from the chair on
which Dr. Clements' clothing was

Dr Houston and Dr and Mrs Clements. (Southport Visiter)

series of unfortunate happenings that had dogged the Clements family for nearly thirty years, but there was one final catastrophe to come. The headline on the front page of the *Southport Visiter* for Tuesday 3 June 1947 read: 'Dramatic New Turn In Southport Mystery. POST MORTEM ON INFIRMARY PATHOLOGIST'. It seems certain that Dr Houston belatedly realised that his error in diagnosing the cause of Amy's death resulted from the fact that he had allowed Clements to influence him with the suggestion that the cause of death was leukaemia. On 2 June, Houston's body was discovered at the infirmary, slumped in an armchair, and the unmistakable smell of bitter almonds indicated that he had taken cyanide. A note lay on the table. It said, 'I have for some time been aware that I have been making mistakes. I have not profited by experience. One just follows another.' His colleagues said that he was a quiet, reserved man, who would have had a brilliant future, but Dr Grace later commented at the coroner's hearing that Houston, who was a diabetic taking insulin, 'was more the research type. I think he was more fitted for that sort of work than the very trying and worrying work in the pathological department of a hospital.'

In due course the inquest resumed, now dealing with three bodies.

Dr Grace's post-mortem reports confirmed that Amy Clements and her husband had both died from morphine poisoning, and that Dr Houston had taken an exceptionally highly concentrated solution of sodium cyanide, very considerably in excess of that required for a fatal dose. There was, he told the court, no evidence of leukaemia in Mrs Clements's body.

The verdict of the coroner's jury was one of murder, against Dr Clements. Two wills made by Clements were found, dated February and March 1944, leaving his estate of £12,000 to his son. Amy Clements seemed to have followed the example of her husband's first three wives and left no will, despite having an estate estimated at £50,000. In view of the coroner's verdict Clements could derive no benefit from his wife's estate, which passed in due course to her near relatives.

Although it is now well over fifty years since these events took place, the affair still lingers in the minds of the Southport medical fraternity. Out of six deaths connected with Clements, four took place in the town and at least one of them, Dr Houston's, could have been prevented. However, it seems some of the people of Southport did not worry too much about that at the time; the *Visiter* dated 3 June 1947 disclosed that for the past two days house-hunters had been arriving at 20 The Promenade, all wanting to take possession of the flat formerly occupied by the unfortunate Amy Clements and her murdering husband.

Dr Clements was interred at Birkdale cemetery on Tuesday 3 June. There were few mourners apart from the dead man's close relatives and only one wreath, a 5ft cross of roses inscribed 'From George and Ernest'. No headstone marks his grave today.

Just before she sailed for Ireland to attend her husband's funeral, Mrs Houston handed a note to the press which said simply, 'My life belonged to my husband – therefore there is nothing more to be said.'

9

DEATH AT THE HOSPITAL

Blackburn, 1948

The busy town of Blackburn sits in a bowl surrounded by moorland, and in 1948 was still dominated by more than fifty giant mill chimneys that reflected the town's dependence on cotton weaving. Blackburn was just beginning to pull itself up by its bootstraps after the war, factory production was on the increase and there was nothing to forecast the devastating collapse of the Lancashire cotton industry that would occur in the mid-1950s. Much of the town consisted of mean terraced streets of two-up, two-down houses, built originally to house the weavers and now reaching the end of their useful lives. Birley Street was such a one, running downhill past the tiny Dutton Arms public house, the street cobbled and virtually empty of vehicular traffic; motor cars were only a dream for the grindingly poor inhabitants.

At no. 31 lived the Griffiths family: Peter Griffiths senior, his wife Elizabeth Alice and their three children James Joseph Brennan (Mrs Griffiths had been married before), Peter Griffiths junior and a daughter, Mary Ellen. James Brennan was himself married, with five children, four of whom were at the time in what would today be known as 'care'. James and his wife were living apart and she was trying to gain control of her children and leave Blackburn for good, which was the subject of regular rows between them. One daughter, Pauline, nearly 3 years old, was convalescing in Blackburn's Queen's Park Hospital on the south-east side of the town. The hospital, a large collection of forbidding-looking brick buildings surrounded by a high stone wall, stood in about seventy acres of land; in the north-west corner the wall had collapsed and was cordoned off by a 6ft-high chestnut paling fence. With little money available during the war and afterwards for refurbishment, the wards were spartan and the three children's wards had little or no decoration to comfort the tiny inhabitants, although the wooden floors were regularly cleaned and polished.

Peter Griffiths junior was aged 22. He was quite tall, 5ft 10½in, slim and

The cobbled Birley Street, where Peter Griffiths lived at no. 31, already a slum in 1948 and demolished twelve years later. (Lancashire Evening Telegraph in conjunction with the Cotton Town project)

not bad looking, although not over-endowed with intelligence. At the age of 6 he had fallen off a milk float, landing on his head, and for some reason his parents did not find out about this accident until a week later. Peter had been sent home from school, sick, and it was one of his schoolmates who finally told Mrs Griffiths about the incident. In those days a visit to the surgery was almost immediately followed by a bill and his parents decided that as their young son appeared to have suffered no harm, it was best to let well alone and not trouble the doctor.

At the age of 8 the boy was admitted to the Queen's Park Hospital suffering from 'incontinence of urine' and he stayed there for the next two years. This would seem to have been an inordinate length of hospitalisation for a young boy who tended to wet his bed, and it is possible that the

Peter Griffiths in his wartime khaki, one
of only two outfits of clothes he possessed.
(popperfoto.com)

'incontinence' masked another and more serious condition. Griffiths himself said that the 'incontinence' soon cleared up and he had no idea why his stay at the hospital was so protracted – there was a suggestion that he might have had tuberculosis, which would have explained his lengthy stay.

After hospital, he had a succession of jobs, none of which lasted long, and he tended to stay indoors shuffling matchboxes around on a table as though they were trains and buses – something which his mother frequently complained about, telling him 'People will think you're mental.' Records at the National Archives disclose that between November 1941 and July 1942 he was in trouble with the law no fewer than four times, receiving twelve months' probation for stealing money, and another two years' probation only three months later for a similar offence. In June 1942 he was fined £2 for housebreaking and larceny, and was back in court seven weeks later to be fined another £2 for taking and driving away a motor lorry without authority. The Blackburn magistrates seem to have been excessively lenient, possibly because of his limited intelligence and poor background.

On 17 February 1944 he was called up into the army and joined the Welsh Guards, seeing service in Europe and Africa before being demobbed in February 1948, with his character assessed as 'Indifferent'. His military service had done little for him except give him a taste for strong drink and he was often to be seen in the Dutton Arms and similar establishments, drinking far more than was good for him or, for that matter, than he could afford. He shared a room at no. 31 with his half-brother, but if James was occupying the room when he came home, he would sleep downstairs fully clothed.

Griffiths had little interest in the normal

occupations of young men of his age, such as football or cricket, and passed the time with his matchboxes and cutting out pictures from newspapers and magazines, which he gummed into a scrapbook. He had struck up a desultory friendship with a local girl, Rene Edge, who worked as a weaver and they would occasionally go to the pictures or for a walk. Rene did not regard herself as Peter's girlfriend although he had proposed marriage to her, which she rejected. The proposal could possibly have been a ruse to persuade the girl to have intercourse with him, as he was later to grumble to the police that 'We talked about having intercourse, but always she jibbed when it came to the point.' By the middle of April 1948 Rene had become concerned about Griffiths's drinking and told him that she would not go out with him any more; but on 10 May the two met accidentally and he asked her to resume the friendship. Once again she refused, possibly a little half-heartedly, as Griffiths appeared not to be able to take 'no' for an answer and she continued to see him at odd intervals thereafter.

On the evening of Friday 14 May taxi-driver Bernard Regan was heading towards the taxi rank by the station, in the centre of town, when he was flagged down by Peter Griffiths, dressed in his blue demob suit. Griffiths wanted to be taken to Queen's Park Hospital (which was in completely the opposite direction to Birley Street) and the time was about 11.50; however, this did not trouble Regan, as it was not unusual for relatives to visit late at night if the matter was urgent. On his own admission, Peter Griffiths had drunk thirteen pints of beer and two double rums that evening and it is surprising that he was in any condition to want to do anything except go home to his bed. The taxi drew up by a small quarry known locally as the Delph, in the area where the hospital wall had collapsed, and after paying the fare of 5s Griffiths ran off into the darkness in the direction of the hospital.

At around 12.30 Nurse Gwendoline Humphreys was washing up in the small kitchen adjoining children's ward CH3. The ward was a rectangular building with large windows and contained twelve tubular metal drop-side cots, six on each side, only half of which were occupied. In the middle of the passageway between the cots were a dressing cabinet, a low table and a trolley. The room could be entered either from the inner door, which led from a corridor to the babies' and toddlers' wards and the sister's office, or from the outside via a small porch whose door was usually kept unlocked at night. To one side of the porch was a small storeroom with three windows, through which entrance could also easily be gained.

About half an hour previously one of the small children had woken up crying and Nurse Humphreys had gone to quieten him. At that time, she said, everything was as it should be. Then she thought she heard a girl's voice in the ward and went to look. Opening the porch door at the far end of the ward the nurse could see nothing, but as she turned to go back into the ward, she noticed that there were three bottles of sterile water on the trolley by the

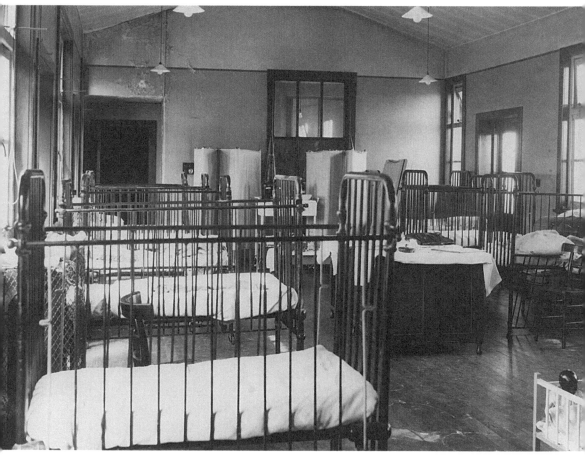

Children's Ward CH3 at Queen's Park Hospital, Blackburn. June Anne Devaney's bed was third on the left. (National Archives)

door. She went back into the kitchen and continued preparing the children's breakfasts. Then she heard another child begin to cry. After about a quarter of an hour, the child settled down and Nurse Humphreys got on with her preparation, walking back into the ward at about 1.15 – immediately noticing that the third cot from the left was empty. It should have been occupied by June Anne Devaney, almost 4 years old but tall for her age; under the cot was one of the Winchester bottles that had a few minutes before been standing on the trolley at the far end of the ward.

It was not possible that June Devaney, tall as she was, could have climbed out of her cot unaided. The increasingly distraught Nurse Humphreys searched the ward and noticed that on the highly polished wooden floor were the marks of stockinged feet, which appeared to run the full length of the room. At the end of the ward the porch door was open, as was one of the three windows in the storeroom. It was soon obvious that June Devaney was not in the ward and Nurse Humphreys hurried for the night sister, who immediately informed her superiors and telephoned the police. Police Constable Edward Parkinson, with some of his colleagues, went to June Devaney's home, 32 Princess Street, Blackburn, to break the news to her father, Albert Devaney, who dressed hurriedly and went with the police to the hospital, where a search was now in full swing.

At 3.15, in the half-light before dawn, little June Anne Devaney's body was found face down, with her nightie up over her waist, lying in the longish grass by the wall, a short distance from the ward. She had been assaulted. There were severe bruises over her face and scalp, and blood coming from her nose and lower parts. There were marks on the ankles, as though caused by fingernails gripping the ankles tightly, and she had been raped. Later, the post-mortem performed by Dr Gilbert Bailey confirmed that the cause of death was shock and haemorrhage caused by two fractures of the skull, consistent with the body having been held by the feet and swung against the stone wall. It was also apparent that the dead girl had been bitten in the lower part of the back. Dr Bailey said that he had been in medical practice for thirty-four years, twenty years as police surgeon, and considered that the injuries must have been committed by someone in a state of maniacal frenzy.

At that time the Blackburn Borough police force was under the command of Chief Constable Cornelius G. Looms; in the early hours of 15 May he telephoned the Chief Constable of Lancashire to ask for the services of a fingerprint expert to help with the investigation. He also had something else to consider – whether or not to call in Scotland Yard. Many forces of the time had neither the skills nor the resources to mount a major murder investigation, although some were just starting to flex their muscles and beginning to think that they were as well equipped to deal with murders as the Met. However, if the Yard was called in quickly it stood the cost of the inquiry, whereas if there was too much delay the cost fell upon the home force, and so Chief Constable Looms quickly made up his mind.

Within hours, Chief Inspector Jack Capstick and his sergeant were at the scene of the crime, and although hardened police officers with many years' service between them, they were devastated by the sight of young June Devaney's injuries. It was obvious that the murderer was a fairly tall man. The footprints on the floor of the ward measured 10½in in length, too big for a woman, and evidence of entry by the damaged wall indicated that the intruder was probably a local. There were clear fingerprints on the water bottle by June Devaney's cot and Capstick surmised that once the fingerprints of the hospital staff had been taken for purposes of elimination, those remaining must belong to the murderer. It was then that he took the momentous decision to fingerprint the entire male population of Blackburn over the age of 16 – a tremendous task and also one of some delicacy. There would almost certainly be an outcry at what many would consider a breach of their citizen's rights, and Capstick decided to approach the Mayor of Blackburn to lead the appeal for volunteers. After some thought the Mayor agreed, but on condition that the prints would be used only to trace the murderer of June Devaney and that once they had served their purpose they would be destroyed. Capstick had no choice but to agree and both the Mayor and the Chief Constable assured the citizens of Blackburn, via the local press, that their interests would be safeguarded.

A plan was drawn up using the electoral registers and teams of police officers, carrying supplies of fingerprint cards and inkpads, worked systematically through the town. It was decided to eliminate first all those people who had had a legitimate reason to be on the hospital premises on the night of the murder, so in due course a team knocked on the door of 31 Birley Street asking to speak to James Brennan, whose daughter had been in the hospital at the time. He gave his fingerprints without demur, watched by his half-brother, who sat sullenly at a table playing with his matchboxes while the procedure was gone through. Altogether it was expected that it might be necessary to take in the region of 40,000 sets of fingerprints from Blackburn residents, and another 3,600 from people who had been discharged from mental institutions in the north of England around the time of the murder – as well as 3,000 prisoners of war and foreign army personnel within a radius of twenty miles of Blackburn, just to be on the safe side.

Two months went by, with thousands of prints being taken without success, and police morale began to drop as day followed day with no result. When 40,000 sets of prints had been examined it began to look as though the murderer might not be a local man after all. The whole of the exercise had been built round just this premise, but there was always the possibility that the perpetrator of the crime was a transient, just passing through, which would mean that the fingerprinting had no chance at all of showing up the culprit. Then someone had a bright idea. The search so far had been based on the electoral roll, but there were some people, including servicemen recently demobbed, who were not currently be registered to vote. Blackburn had recently issued new ration books to its citizens and when the electoral roll was compared with the records kept by the Local Registration Officer, there were some 200 people missing. It did not take long for the police to visit the 'missing' people and a few days later, fingerprint set number 46253 proved to be a match for the prints on the water bottle. The name on the card was Peter Griffiths, of 31 Birley Street.

On the evening of Friday 13 August 1948 Griffiths left his house and was walking down Birley Street when he was stopped by Inspectors Capstick and Barton. 'We are police officers,' said Barton. 'I am arresting you for the murder of June Anne Devaney at Queen's Park Hospital on 14 or 15 May this year.'

'What is it to do with me?' muttered the young man, who was wearing his army battledress, his only outer clothing apart from the blue demob suit that had been pawned by his mother on 30 May. She had never since had the money to redeem it and it was still at the pawnbrokers, heavily bloodstained, something that had presumably been missed by both Mrs Griffiths and the pawnbroker. Griffiths denied to the arresting officers that he had ever been near the hospital, but in the car on the way to Blackburn police station he volunteered that he had been in Queen's Park Hospital as a boy, and then said almost as an afterthought, 'Is it my fingerprints why you came to me?' When told that it was, he went on, 'Well, if they are my fingerprints on the bottle, I'll tell you all about it.'

Capstick, Barton and Detective Sergeant Mullen faced Griffiths in the interview room and after cautioning him, Mullen wrote down the young man's statement:

I want to say that on the night the little girl was killed at the Queen's Park Hospital, it was on a Friday night, the Friday before Whitsun. I left home on my own about six o'clock to spend a quiet night by myself. I went to the Dun Horse pub and bought myself about five pints of bitter beer, then I went to Yates's Wine Lodge and had a glass of Guinness and two double rums. I then had another glass of Guinness and then went back to the Dun Horse again. I then had six more pints of bitter. I was on my own and came out of there at closing time. I walked down to Jubilee Street, off Darwen Street and I saw a man smoking a cigarette sitting in a small closed car with the hood on, with wire wheels, they were painted silver. I did not know him, I had never seen him before. I asked the man for a light, as I had no matches to light my cigarette. I stayed gabbing to him for about fifteen minutes, he said to me 'Are you going home?' I said, 'No. I'm going to walk around a bit and sober up first.' He asked me where I lived and I told him. He said, 'Well get in, open the window and I'll give you a spin.' He took me to the front of the hospital and I got out opposite to the iron railings. I don't know what happened to him. I never saw him again. I must have got over the railings, but the next thing I remember was being outside the ward where there was [sic] some children. I left my shoes outside a door which had a brass knob. I tried the door and it opened to my touch and I went just in and I heard a nurse humming and banging things as if she was washing something so I came out again and waited a few minutes. Then I went back in again and went straight in the ward like, I think I went in one or two small rooms, like a kitchen, and then came back into the ward again. I then picked up a biggish bottle off a shelf. I went halfway down the ward with it and then put it down on the floor. I then thought I heard the nurse coming. I turned round sharply, overbalanced and fell against a bed.

The entrance to Ward CH3. Note the brass knob described by Peter Griffiths. (National Archives)

I remember the child woke up and started to cry and I hushed her, she then opened her eyes and saw me and the child in the next bed started whimpering. I picked the girl up out of the cot and took her outside by the same door. I carried her in my right arm and she put her arms round my neck and I walked with her down the hospital field. I put her down on the grass. She started crying again and I tried to stop her from crying but she wouldn't do like, she wouldn't stop crying. I just lost my temper then. I banged her head against the wall. I then went back to the veranda outside the ward, sat down and put my shoes on. I then went back to where the child was. I like just glanced at her but did not go right up to her but went straight on down the field to the Delph. I crossed over the path alongside the Delph leading in to Queen's Park and came out on Audley. I went down Cherry Street into Furthergate, then I went down Eanam to Birley Street and got home somewhere around 2 o'clock on Saturday morning. It would be somewhere about that time. I went in my house, took my collar and tie off and slept in my suit on the couch downstairs. Mother and father were in bed and did not know what time I came in. I woke up about 9 o'clock, got up, washed and shaved, then pressed my suit because I was going out again after I had had my breakfast. I went out then down the town, had a walk round then went to the Royal cinema afternoon, came out of the pictures at 5 o'clock, went home and had my tea. I looked at the papers and read about the murder, it didn't shake me so that I just carried on normally after that. My mother and father asked me where I had been that night and what time I came home and I told them I had been out boozing and had got home at 12 o'clock. This is all I can say and I'm sorry for both parents' sake and I hope I get what I deserve.

This amazing statement, produced as Exhibit 9 at the trial, bears closer consideration. It is amazingly detailed in parts and vague in others. For instance, would this uneducated young man have appreciated, three months after the event, that his crime was committed 'on the Friday before Whitsun'? And, given the amount of alcohol he had consumed, which would have rendered many a man comatose, what was the point of the description of the car belonging to the man who had picked him up 'for a spin', and that later turned out to be a figment of his imagination? Griffiths, in his befuddled alcoholic state, could seemingly remember every little move once he got to the hospital, including the fact that the porch door had a brass knob. Pointedly, he made no mention in his statement of the reason for his having decided to go to the hospital in the first place so late at night, more than twice as far from his home as the point where he boarded the taxi and in the opposite direction. He described picking up June Anne Devaney, taking her outside and becoming annoyed because of her crying, but not a word about the horrific sexual attack on the defenceless 3-year-old, which left her ravaged and bleeding before being cruelly battered to death. It is perhaps not surprising that he either could not, or preferred not to, remember those horrendous few minutes of pointless ferocity.

His confession that on the following day he had no 'untoward feelings' when he read the newspapers, which were full of the murder, again smacks of an attempt to blot the facts from his memory, although when questioned by his parents he lied about the time he got home, which would indicate that he knew he had done something that needed to be lied about. From then on he carried on as usual and continued to drink in the local pubs, even resuming his desultory relationship with Rene Edge on 16 May, when she jokingly asked him where he had been the night before. He told her that he had had a few drinks and had gone home to bed around 10.45 – another lie. In a hospital case paper concerning his mental state, made while he was on remand, Griffiths said that he had tried to force himself on Rene around about that time and that she had resisted, telling him that he had a split mind. It might well have been this incident, plus his drinking, which made her tell him for a second time that she did not wish to go out with him any more.

The trial opened on 15 October 1948 before Mr Justice Oliver; Griffiths's defence counsel, Basil Neild KC, MP and Jack de V. Nahum, knew from the start that they had an almost impossible job. Their client had clearly confessed to killing June Devaney and forensic evidence produced to the court only reinforced this. Apart from the damning fingerprints, fibres removed from the window at the hospital were identical to those from the bloodstained blue suit, as were fibres taken from June Devaney's body and nightdress. The footprints on the ward floor also yielded fibres which matched those in a sock removed from the accused's home, and the bloodstains on the suit were of blood group A, the same as the dead girl. The only possible defence was insanity; a decision was made not to put the accused into the witness box and to plead 'guilty but insane'. Evidence was given that Peter Griffiths's father had been an inmate of Prestwich Mental Hospital for six months, albeit thirty years previously, but he did not seem to have had any further history of mental illness since then – although Mrs Griffiths admitted in court that he had claimed he was acting as a 'police spy', listening at doors in an attempt to catch people playing cards. Attempts were made to show that Griffiths was a paranoid schizophrenic, a condition possibly inherited from his father, the defence claiming that the incontinence of urine, lack of friends and the solitary playing with matchboxes were all signs of early schizophrenia. However, the testimony of Dr Francis Herbert Brisby, the Principal Medical Officer at Liverpool Prison, now contained in the trial papers at the National Archives, showed that he had had Griffiths under observation for upwards of two months and had found no evidence of any disease of the mind which would have prevented him from either knowing what he was doing, or that it was wrong.

The jury took just twenty-five minutes to find Peter Griffiths guilty and the judge solemnly pronounced sentence of death. The accused paid no attention to what the judge was saying and it was doubtful, so an onlooker said, whether he heard a word that was said to him.

On 4 November the Home Secretary ordered a medical inquiry under Section (24) of the Criminal Lunatics Act 1884 into the mental condition of the condemned man. It was conducted by Sir Norwood East, formerly medical commissioner of HM Prisons, Dr J.S.Hopwood of Broadmoor Criminal Lunatic Asylum and Dr Young, Director of Medical Services for HM Prisons. They noted that Griffiths asked for, and was given, ten cigarettes a day while in the condemned cell, that he was a little below normal intelligence, and they agreed with the assessment of Dr Brisby. They also agreed with the conclusions of the Roman Catholic chaplain at Liverpool Prison that Griffiths was purposely untruthful and, though they accepted that he had been drinking heavily on the night of the murder, they did not consider that this prevented him from knowing what he was doing or knowing that it was wrong. Griffiths's patchy memory was deemed to be a defensive reaction, possibly affected by the amount that he had had to drink. On 9 November Mr F.A. Newsham wrote from the Home Office to say that: 'Having carefully considered all the circumstances of the case of Peter Griffiths, and having caused a special medical enquiry as to the prisoner's condition to be made . . . the Secretary of State has been unable to find any sufficient ground to justify him in advising His Majesty to interfere with the due course of law.'

Two days before the execution was due to take place, Chief Inspector Capstick was given special permission to interview Griffiths regarding the murder of a young boy named Jack Quentin Smith who, on 12 April, had been stabbed to death at Farnworth, just a few miles from Blackburn. Griffiths agreed to stand in an identity parade, where 12-year-old David Lee, who had been stabbed nine times by Smith's killer and survived, failed to pick him out of a line of nine men. The execution date was set for Friday 19 November 1948 and on the afternoon of the 18th, executioner Albert Pierrepoint and his assistant, Harry Allen, walked quietly to Walton Jail and started their preparations for the following morning. The drop of 7ft 5in was carefully entered in Pierrepoint's execution book and, so Pierrepoint said later, Griffiths died 'like a soldier'.

Shortly afterwards, Chief Constable Looms, assisted by the Mayor of Blackburn, presided over the pulping of the fingerprint cards at the Richmond Hill Paper Works, watched by assorted journalists and a newsreel camera crew. Those who had given fingerprints were offered the chance to retain their cards and about 500 people accepted the opportunity.

For years afterwards, on the anniversary of her death, June Anne Devaney's family placed an 'In Memoriam' notice in the *Northern Daily Telegraph*.

10

A POISONOUS COUPLE

Blackpool, 1953

Louisa May Merrifield lived a hard life. Born in 1907, she was brought up in a God-fearing Methodist home alongside her four sisters, although little of the Good Word seems to have rubbed off on her. Never a particularly good-looking girl, short and dumpy even in her teens and just 5ft tall, Louisa left marriage till she was 25, in 1932 wedding Joseph Ellison, a foundryman, with whom she had two sons and two daughters. Married life was a struggle; Joseph was never a well man and the children were in and out of local authority care all the time. Louisa herself fell foul of the law in 1946 when she served a total of eighty-four days in prison for being in possession of forged ration books. She took her incarceration with her usual phlegmatic calm.

By 1949, although the war had ended four years previously, many things were still on ration and the populace as a whole was underfed, clothes were drab and it was still considered sinful to go to the cinema on Sunday evenings. The trams bore notices warning against spitting – penalty 40s – and a trip on the upper deck at rush hour was not a pleasant experience. Few public houses catered for young people, most being frequented by war veterans and old men, and they were not generally considered respectable places for a young woman to visit. This did not trouble Louisa though, who despite her chapel upbringing could swear and tell rude jokes with the best of them. Entertainment of a sort, consisting of social evenings and the 'Ladies Bright Hour' was provided by the chapel, but unfortunately for Louisa the Methodists did not believe in dancing or drinking, two of her favourite pastimes – so she left their austere number and transferred to the Salvation Army, who took a more broad-minded attitude to sinners.

Joseph died the same year, supposedly of a diseased liver, and barely three months later Louisa married her lodger, Richard Weston. Weston was 78 and in poor health; not surprisingly he soon passed away, leaving Louisa a widow for the second time. She married again, this time 67-year-old Alfred Merrifield, who was small but always well dressed, and who invariably carried a silver-topped cane whenever he went out. He was also very deaf and

An unsmiling Mrs Merrifield and her 'tragic simpleton' of a husband. (popperfoto.com)

sported an enormous hearing aid, but this handicap was alleviated in Louisa's eyes by the fact of his having his old-age pension and savings of around £350; he was also fit and well for his age. Why he should have been attracted to the hatchet-faced Louisa is unclear, but perhaps it was because he could see that her energy and his income would ensure that they always had a roof over their heads.

Despite Alfred's modest income, it was still necessary for the two of them to earn extra cash to survive in comfort, and for a while they tried to run a small, rented boarding house. This failed, however, taking with it most of Alfred's hard-won nest-egg, after which they had a succession of small, poorly paid jobs that just about kept the wolf from the door. In November 1952 the Merrifields were lodging at 33 Alexandra Road, Blackpool, with Mrs Elizabeth Heywood (who complained that when they left her they also left unpaid a bill of nearly £6 for coal); and by early 1953, their fortunes not improving, they were once again looking round for another position.

The sought-for improvement in their circumstances came via an advertisement in the local paper, the *West Lancashire Evening Gazette*, placed by a Mrs Sarah Ricketts, who lived in a small but well-built, two-bedroomed bungalow called The Homestead at 339 Devonshire Road, Blackpool. The advertisement, in the 'situations vacant' column, read: 'HOUSEKEEPER/ COMPANION for one lady, small, modern and attractive home in Norbreck. References essential. Car driver an advantage. Age 35 to 50.' In her youth Sarah Ricketts had been a good-looking girl, much in demand by the local lads, but she had been twice widowed and at the age of 79 was living out her final years in modest comfort in the seaside resort. Only 4ft 8in inches tall, she was very frail, with a withered arm that made it difficult for her to look after herself. She also had a temper and neither of her two daughters visited her very often. One, who rejoiced in the name of Loveday Whittaker, confessed in her statement to the police that 'Mother and I on occasions had rather slight differences of opinion . . . she was rather difficult sometimes to get on with.'

The advertisement drew more than fifty replies but, perhaps sensing a kindred spirit in the much-married Mrs Merrifield, Sarah Ricketts offered her the job. There is some doubt whether Mrs Ricketts knew about Alfred when she made her choice, but he was soon on the scene and the old lady grumbled that he did little but sit about the house all day, 'cluttering the place up'. The agreement was that the Merrifields would receive no payment for their services and their electricity, gas and food would all have to be paid for, but they were to live at The Homestead rent free, which for the moment was good enough for them. They might perhaps not have been so pleased had they known a little more about the history of 339 Devonshire Road, which had seen the deaths of Sarah's two husbands, both of whom had committed suicide by gassing themselves in the kitchen.

At first the elderly invalid was more than satisfied with her guests and indeed, started to worry in case they decided to leave her. She kept mainly to her bed, eating spoonfuls of jam in between sipping eggcups of brandy and began to hint that she would, if treated nicely, make a will in their favour, leaving them the bungalow, then worth around £3,000. Louisa, sensing that their fortunes were on the upturn, promptly devoted extra care and attention to their benefactor. Within weeks a will had been drawn up, although Mrs Ricketts delayed signing it, using this as a small stick to encourage further efforts from her live-in guests. It was drawn up in favour of Louisa alone, whether by accident or design, but Alfred, 'not being as green as he was cabbage looking' – to use a Lancashire phrase – soon found out and insisted that his name was added. The solicitor, Mr W.A. Darbyshire, did not bother to go to the trouble of drawing up a new document but merely added '*Alfred Edward Merrifield and*' in writing to the typewritten will, the alteration being initialled by him, his clerk Clara Marchant and Mrs Ricketts. At the same time Alfred joined his wife as an executor of the will, which was dated 31 March 1953 and stipulated that on the death of the testator the Merrifields were to receive 'all my property both real and personal whatsoever and wheresoever', no provision being made for either of the testator's daughters.

Aside from the gruesome fate of her unfortunate husbands, Sarah Ricketts had another little secret, in that it was not the first time she had used The Homestead in this fashion to keep her carers sweet. More than once she had promised to leave the bungalow to the person who was looking after her at the time, although this munificence never lasted long and, true to form, she was soon beginning to grow disenchanted with the Merrifields. Only days after the will had been signed, she began to complain to visiting tradesmen that the Merrifields were spending her money like water. Louisa, it seemed, was not above adding a bottle or two of the hard stuff to the weekly shopping list, which fact had not gone unnoticed by the eagle-eyed old lady, and she told a delivery man who called with a bottle of rum on 13 April, 'I don't know what they are doing with my money . . . they will have to go.'

Whatever else Louisa was, she was a good talker and she tried her best to keep the cantankerous old woman sweet. Learning that Mrs Ricketts was favourably inclined towards the Salvation Army, she suddenly recalled her own short flirtation with them, which impressed and reassured the old lady for the time being. There was now only one fly in the ointment – Sarah Ricketts was old and frail and although the will had been drawn up perfectly legally, Louisa was certain that the two daughters would protest once they found out that all their mother's estate had gone to strangers. She was cunning enough to know that the best way forward was to get a doctor to certify that Mrs Ricketts was of sound mind when she made her will, and so on 9 April she approached Dr Yule, who lived only half a mile away in Warbreck Hill Road. She told the somewhat puzzled doctor, who had never seen her or Mrs Ricketts before, that she was concerned to establish that her employer was of sound mind when she made her will and the doctor explained that he could do nothing without examining Mrs Ricketts, arranging to call the following day. When he did so, he was surprised to find an irate Sarah Ricketts, who insisted that she would not submit to any examination and demanded that he leave immediately. Four days later Mrs Merrifield again called on the doctor to discuss the matter, but once Dr Yule discovered that Louisa had no intention of paying his bill, he threw her out.

Louisa took this in her stride, as always. She was full of excitement at the way that providence had brought her to Mrs Ricketts's front door, and even more so at the thought that the front door would be hers in the not-too-distant future – surely the old lady could not last for too much longer? So obsessed was she by her good fortune that she felt constrained to tell the news to anybody who would listen, and when the ink was hardly dry on the will she wrote to a former employer, Mrs Norah Lowe (one of the few with whom she was still on good terms), telling her the story of the 'lovely little bungalow' that an old lady had left her and 'Thank God for it!' She also took the opportunity to ask Mrs Lowe whether she had any old clothes that she would like to sell, as Louisa could not afford to buy new ones. The need for money was evidently pressing.

At the beginning of April she met an old acquaintance, David Brindley, in the street, keeping him standing there until he had been forced to listen to her good-luck story; and on 12 April, coming across another friend, Mrs Jessie Brewer, she exclaimed, 'We're landed! We went to live with an old woman and she died, leaving us a bungalow worth £3,000.' She went on to say that she was thinking of raising a mortgage on the bungalow so that she could buy a small nursing home, and grumbled that her husband – whom she described as 'that old bugger' – had interfered and had persuaded Mrs Ricketts to divide the property between them.

The next day, while deliveryman George Forjan was in the bungalow, Mrs Ricketts asked Alfred Merrifield to go to the bank to withdraw some money, and at the same time she told him that she also wanted him to go to her solicitor because she wished to change her will again, muttering to Forjan that the Merrifields were keeping her short of food and that she was thinking of asking them to leave. Needless to say, Alfred was most reluctant to go on this errand and grumbled that it was too far for him to walk. That same afternoon Louisa was waiting at a bus stop after doing some shopping in Blackpool and, voluble as ever, mentioned to her neighbour in the queue that she had recently been to Wigan to see her son and on her return she had found her husband in bed with Mrs Ricketts. 'If it happens again, I'll poison the old bugger and him as well,' she remarked to her bewildered fellow passenger. 'She was leaving the bungalow between me and my husband, but he's so greedy he wants it all on his own.'

Later in the evening Louisa telephoned the local surgery, seeking a doctor and saying that the old lady was seriously ill. Dr Albert Wood, who was not very well himself but was used to the frail Mrs Ricketts and her tantrums, did not relish making a home call so late and grumbled, 'Won't it wait until the morning?' 'What happens if she dies in the night?' was the sharp reply. Reluctantly, Dr Wood arrived at The Homestead and knocked on the door, which was opened by Louisa. To his annoyance, he found Mrs Ricketts a little shaky, but otherwise all right and prescribed a mild sedative, spending a few minutes with her in private conversation before making for the door, where Louisa buttonholed him and mentioned the will. Protesting that he did not want to get involved with his patient's domestic affairs, he left. The following morning Louisa again phoned the surgery asking for a house call, as Mrs Ricketts was now much worse. Dr Wood, having made one wasted call, was reluctant to make another and sent his partner, Dr Page, instead. The old lady lay in bed, plainly near her end, while Alfred Merrifield was calmly eating his lunch at a table that had been pushed up against the bed. Page saw immediately that it was too late for him to do anything for the old woman and sent for Dr Yule, but by the time he arrived Mrs Ricketts was dead. Yule emphatically refused to sign the death certificate. Under the circumstances, he insisted, a post-mortem would have to be carried out and the coroner advised, especially as Mrs Merrifield seemed anxious that her former employer should be cremated as soon as possible.

The news of the death was carried in the local newspapers and the report was seen by, among others, Mrs Brewer. She realised that at the time of her conversation with the loquacious Mrs Merrifield, Sarah Ricketts had still been very much alive, and so she promptly telephoned the police to see if the newspaper account of Mrs Ricketts's death was correct. Meanwhile, the post-mortem had been carried out and pathologist Dr G.B. Manning submitted that Mrs Ricketts's stomach contained a mixture of brandy and bran – the latter being a constituent of a well-known rat poison called 'Rodine' – and that death was due to phosphorus poisoning. Mrs Ricketts had almost certainly been murdered and the Chief Constable of Blackpool Borough police, Harry Barnes, decided that his force would be out of their depth in this case, where direct evidence was more or less non-existent. He called in Scotland Yard, who sent Detective Superintendent Colin McDougall to take charge of the investigation. Within a short time the police were at the bungalow questioning the Merrifields, especially as to whether either of them had bought any rat poison, which they both denied. The police then carried out a systematic examination of the bungalow and were soon digging up the front garden, calmly watched by Louisa and Alfred, who told them that their late employer

Ever willing to be photographed, even when the police were closing in on her, Mrs Merrifield did her housework for the cameras. (popperfoto.com)

was given to heavy drinking of brandy and that she used to partake of an egg-and-brandy mixture at least three times a day, a potion that she always mixed herself.

The press had arrived in some numbers and perched themselves on the garden wall, watching the perspiring policemen at their digging and noting that Louisa frequently offered them cups of tea – which just as frequently they refused! If the police would not pay her any attention, the gentlemen of the press certainly were prepared to and they took great care to humour her, carefully writing in their notebooks every word she uttered and taking photographs as she went about her household duties. Louisa appeared to have no idea of the awkward, not to say dangerous, position she and Alfred were in, and soon the journalists were delighting in her account of the will and how they would now be able to live in modest comfort for the rest of their lives – although she did vouchsafe that 'I have an enemy in this town, who is trying to make my life difficult.'

On 30 April the police arrested Mrs Merrifield, charging her with the murder of Mrs Ricketts, and for once she was speechless – but recovered sufficiently to wave cheerfully to the press photographers who clustered round the police car taking her to Strangeways Prison. Two days later, the town was in a foment as Stanley Matthews scored the goal that won the Wembley Cup Final for Blackpool, 4–3 against Bolton, and for a short time the Merrifields vanished from the front pages.

The front room of Mrs Ricketts's bungalow. The front-page headline on the copy of the Gazette lying on the table reads 'Mr MERRIFIELD ACCUSED OF MURDER – Arrested after going to see wife in cell'. (National Archives)

Alfred continued to stay at the bungalow, fending for himself and maintaining his perpetual vacant grin, but during one of his visits to Louisa, on 14 May, he was suddenly arrested and, to his indignation, charged with murder alongside his wife. Both pleaded 'Not Guilty' and the preliminary hearing commenced at Blackpool Magistrates Court.

No trace of poison had been found in or around the bungalow, but John Budd, the solicitor acting for Mrs Merrifield, caused a minor sensation when he announced to the court that he was in possession of 'certain objects' which had been handed to him by Alfred Merrifield at an interview during which the old man had been seeking legal advice. Merrifield told the lawyer that a brown handbag had been left by Louisa with an acquaintance of hers, Mrs Alice Cawton, on 14 April, to await collection by a friend. Louisa had told Mrs Cawton that she was in trouble as 'the old lady had died without a doctor'. The bag was supposed to contain life policies on Alfred's life which Louisa did not want him to know about, but on 4 May Alfred called to see Mrs Cawton, who did not demur when he took the bag away with him. Mr Budd claimed that the 'objects' were the subject of privilege between himself and his client, a proposal that was accepted by the magistrates but later overturned. Upon examination, the bag was found to contain fragments of toffee papers, hairs and fibres and an ordinary household dessert spoon which a forensic report, issued by Dr Firth, Head of the North West Forensic Science Laboratory, stated had a 'thin, sticky, colourless deposit on the bowl, adhering to which were fragments of tobacco and paper'. Dr Firth said that there was no odour and he could not find any evidence of Rodine rat poison on the spoon, but the sticky deposit was soluble in water and gave a reaction for sugars.

The only real evidence against the Merrifields, it seemed, was circumstantial. Mrs Ricketts had undoubtedly been poisoned and the Merrifields were the obvious people to have administered it, having had both motive and opportunity; but there was no proof that they had ever possessed any Rodine and neither had any been found on the premises. Despite this lack of hard evidence the Merrifields were committed for trial, which began at Manchester Assizes on Monday 20 July 1953. The public gallery was full, many people having queued overnight to ensure a good seat, and the presiding judge was Mr Justice Glyn-Jones, conducting his first capital trial and probably chosen because he was a fully qualified chemist. The prosecution was led by the Attorney General, Sir Lionel Heald QC, as was normal in poisoning cases, and Mr Jack Nahum QC represented the Merrifields. He could see from the start that he had a formidable task on his hands – one client was garrulous in the extreme and seemed to revel in the situation, wearing a dove-grey hat and coat and having had her hair freshly permed for the occasion, while the other was an imbecile. Alfred wore a brown suit with striped shirt and stiff white collar and seemed more concerned with waving to the members of the press in their box than he did with attending to what was going on around him. Before her arrest Louisa had been prepared to talk to everyone and anyone, and now she seemed very confident that she would be acquitted. Nahum had been at pains to get over to her that the atmosphere in the courtroom would be far different from the four-ale bar to which she was more accustomed, and that merry banter and coarse jokes would not be appreciated: but still she persisted in her irrational cheerfulness.

The Attorney General tried to make the best of a thin case by suggesting to the jury that the spoon found in Louisa Merrifield's handbag had been washed clean (something that was negated by Dr Firth's evidence), and that if she was innocent she would have had no reason to destroy the evidence. This supposed that the poison had actually been administered by spoon, something of which there was no evidence whatsoever. Dr George Manning again submitted that Mrs Ricketts had died from phosphorus administered on the evening of 13 April and that the phosphorus most probably came from Rodine, the well-known form of rat poison. It was highly poisonous, a fatal dose being as little as 65 milligrams (about 1 grain), and a small tin of Rodine on its own contained about 10 grains. The symptoms of phosphorus poisoning were nausea, a burning sensation in the throat and vomiting, accompanied by intense thirst; death sometimes occurred within twenty-four hours, although it could extend to several days. He estimated that only 0.141 of a grain of the poison remained in the body of the deceased, but Dr Firth later pointed out that it was not to be implied that a fatal dose would necessarily be found in the body after death, owing to vomiting.

Evidence for the defence came from the well-respected Professor J.N. Webster, Director of the Home Office Laboratory at Birmingham and Professor of Forensic Medicine at Birmingham University, who, while admitting that the deceased might well have taken phosphorus, opined that she could possibly have died from cirrhosis of the liver before the poison could take effect. The judge was somewhat incredulous at this suggestion, and made it clear to the court that he did not think much of it. However, in view of Professor Webster's reputation, it was an important point for the defence, alongside the fact that no poison or poison container had been found in the bungalow and there was also no evidence to tie the Merrifields in with Rodine at all.

A Mr Roland Wright, pharmacist of 49 Forshaw Avenue, Blackpool, stated that between 14 and 20 March a woman came into his shop and bought a shilling tin of Rodine. He described her as being about 50, 5ft to 5ft 2in tall at the most, fairly well built and wearing glasses, a description that could possibly have applied to Mrs Merrifield; but Mr Wright had also had ample opportunity to see pictures of her in the newspapers, and the judge emphasised

*A seemingly confident and smiling Mrs Merrifield on her way back to Strangeways Prison,
after the third day of the hearing.* (popperfoto.com)

in his summing up that this particular piece of evidence was worthless and the
jury were to disregard it. The prosecution also put up Edith Cummins, the
manageress of a chemist's shop in Crumpsall, Manchester, who told the court
that she remembered selling a tin of Rodine to an elderly man, but she could
recall neither the date nor whether the man was wearing a hearing aid and
carrying a stick. One wonders why this evidence was put forward, as it tended
to diminish the force of the prosecution's case and the jury could perhaps
have been forgiven for wondering whether the prosecution was so hard up for
evidence that it was desperate to try anything.

It was then time for Mrs Merrifield to 'have her day', as she put it to her
cell-mates in Strangeways Prison; confident that she would carry all before

her, she boasted that she would not be coming back to her cell once she had a chance to tell the court her side of the story. She was in the dock for over nine hours, spread over three days – a considerable amount of time to face hostile questioning of her every movement and she stood the ordeal well, although her demeanour did not create a favourable impression on judge or jury. She adopted the position that all the evidence against her was a matter of gossip. When questioned about the numerous conversations she had had, some with complete strangers, often asserting that her benefactor had died and left her the bungalow when Mrs Ricketts was still very much alive, she scoffed, 'It's just jealousy. They are all up to their necks in mortgages.' She also flatly denied ever having told anyone that Mrs Ricketts was dead before the event. When questioned about the spoon that had been found in her handbag, she claimed that she had moved house on so many occasions that she often had items of cutlery in her handbag. She was conscious, too, of the fact that although the spoon had been closely examined, no trace of poison had been found on it.

She claimed to have loved the late Mrs Ricketts (as well she might, seeing that she was to inherit a large part of the old woman's estate), and that on the fatal evening she had been up all night nursing her charge. She averred that Mrs Ricketts had vomited and had suffered intense thirst and pain in the abdomen, and that she had given Mrs Ricketts a drink from an eggcup full of brandy that she said had been 'mixed' by the old lady. The Attorney General leapt on this slip at once. 'Mixed with what?' he queried. 'I don't know,' was the firm reply, 'Mrs Ricketts always prepared the drink herself before she went to bed, and put it on the bedside table.'

The reasons put forward for why no doctor had been called during the night, when it was admitted that Mrs Ricketts was seriously ill and partly comatose, were lame and did the Merrifields no favours in the courtroom. Mrs Merrifield claimed that she did not like to go out so late at night, and her husband was content to say that he was too crippled to walk all that way. When questioned, however, he was forced to admit that he could walk to the bus stop, which was further away than the doctor's house. Mrs Merrifield gave evidence that 'I was up and down with her five or six times during the night . . . she went to the toilet and cried, saying to me, "You don't know how ill I am." I got her into bed and she seemed a little quieter and the next thing I heard she was up again and in the hall on the floor. I got her into bed and she thanked me and my husband for what we had done for her. Those were her last words.' Alfred Merrifield repeated his wife's story about Sarah Ricketts's last illness and stoutly denied that he had ever had any Rodine or that he had given any to the deceased. His evidence was given in a firm voice, although he did occasionally have trouble with his hearing aid, and Mr Nahum referred to him in his closing speech as 'this tragic simpleton'.

This is the last Will of me

SARAH ANN RICKETTS of 399 Devonshire Road Blackpool in the County of Lancaster Widow which I make this *Thirty first* day of *March* one thousand nine hundred and fifty three hereby revoking all other wills and testamentary dispositions by me heretofore made

SUBJECT to the payment of my funeral and testamentary expenses death duties and debts I give all my property both real and personal whatsoever and wheresoever situate to *Alfred Edward Merrifield and* Louisa Merrifield of 399 Devonshire Road Blackpool aforesaid absolutely and I appoint *them* to be the ~~sole executrix~~ *executors* of this my Will

IN WITNESS whereof I the said Sarah Ann Ricketts have to this my Will set my hand the day and year first before written

S. A. Ricketts.

SIGNED by the above named Testatrix as her last Will in the presence of us both present at the same time who in her presence at her request and in the presence of each other have hereunto subscribed our names as witnesses

W. Arnold Derbyshire
Solicitor
Blackpool
Clara Marchant
His Clerk.

The amended will which left everything to the Merrifields. (National Archives)

The trial ended after eleven days, on 31 July. The judge summed up, taking four hours to review the evidence both for and against the Merrifields and, although he referred to Louisa as 'a vulgar and stupid woman with a dirty mind', he charged the jury that this did not necessarily mean she was guilty of murder. The jury took just six hours to bring in a guilty verdict against Mrs Merrifield who, pulling her right hand free from the restraining grip of the prison warder standing by her side, raised it stiffly in what was to the public gallery strongly reminiscent of a Nazi salute, her mouth firmly shut. The arm was forced down and she was led, without a further word, to the cells below, while Alfred remained to hear what the jury had to say about him. Perhaps affected by his unfortunate manner of making inappropriate jokes in the courtroom and his huge hearing aid, which gave the impression that he was not entirely all there, the jury were unable to agree and Alfred was remanded for retrial.

Mrs Merrifield's appeal was lost and she was hanged at Strangeways Prison on 18 September 1953, aged 46, by Albert Pierrepoint assisted by Jack Stewart. Pierrepoint recorded in his execution book that she weighed 187lb and was given a drop of 8ft 9in. Stewart later recalled in his diary, 'It went better than I had imagined. She was braver than any man. The female officers on watch appeared a trifle upset.'

The Attorney General decided that he would not prosecute Albert a second time and he was released, immediately attempting to claim his inheritance under the will. Mrs Ricketts's two daughters fought hard to prevent this and eventually, after remaining in the bungalow for three more years, Merrifield had to be satisfied with a one-sixth share of the estate amounting to just £209, legal fees having taken a large portion of the inheritance. A year later, he was again in the news when Fylde Rural District Council attempted to remove him from a small plot on a caravan site near Blackpool, where he had been living for some time and had also bought a second caravan which he rented out to holidaymakers. A newspaper quoted him as saying, 'I have had my share of trouble. I don't want any more.' Eventually, after being reduced to exhibiting himself in a Blackpool sideshow, he died at the age of 80 in 1962.

BIBLIOGRAPHY

ABBREVIATIONS

PRO – Public Record Office (now the National Archives)

1. STEEPED IN ARSENIC

PRO, HO 144/1638/A50678
PRO, HO 144/539/A50678F, E & H
Notable British Trials series: *Mrs Maybrick*, Irving, H.B. (ed.), Hodge 1912
Farrell, Michael, *Poisons and Poisoners*, Hale 1992
Green, Jonathan, *The Directory of Infamy*, Mills & Boon 1980
Harrison, Shirley (ed.), *The Diary of Jack the Ripper*, BCA 1993
Morland, Nigel, *This Friendless Lady*, Muller 1957
Ryan, Bernard, *The Poisoned Life of Mrs Maybrick*, William Kimber 1977
Search, Pamela (ed.), *Great True Crime Stories (Women)*, Arco 1957
Watson, Katherine, *Poisoned Lives*, Hambledon 2004

2. THE BODY IN THE WARDROBE

Accrington Observer
Bury Times

3. TRIPLE MURDER

PRO, ASSI 52/170
Jackson, Stanley, *Mr Justice Avory*, Gollancz 1935

4. THE BRIDES IN THE BATH

PRO, DPP/1/43
PRO, MEPO 3/225B
Notable British Trials series: *George Joseph Smith*, Watson, Eric R. (ed.),
   Hodge 1922
Bolitho, William, *Murder for Profit*, Jonathan Cape 1926
Browne, Douglas G., *Sir Travers Humphries – A Biography*, Harrap 1960
—— and Tullett, Tom, *Bernard Spilsbury: His Life and Cases*, Harrap 1951
La Bern, Arthur, *Life and Death of a Ladykiller*, Leslie Frewin 1967
Lyons, F.J., *George Joseph Smith*, Duckworth 1935
Meadley, R. (ed.), *Classics in Murder*, Xanadu 1984

5. The Man from the Pru

PRO, HO 144/17738, 17739
Agate, James, *Ego 6*, Harrap 1944
Brophy, L., *The Meaning of Murder*, Whiting & Wheaton 1966
Goodman, Jonathan, *The Killing of Julia Wallace*, Harrap 1969
Hussey, Robert F., *Murderer: Scot Free*, David & Charles 1972
Lustgarten, Edgar, *The Murder and The Trial*, Odhams 1960
——, *Verdict in Dispute*, Wingate 1949
Murphy, James, *The Murder of Julia Wallace*, Bluecoat Press 2001
Rowland, John, *The Wallace Case*, Carroll & Nicholson 1949
Shew, E. Spencer, *A Second Companion to Murder*, Cassell 1962
Whittington-Egan, Richard, *Tales of Liverpool Murder, Mayhem and Mystery*, Gallery Press 1967
Wilkes, Roger, *Wallace: The Final Verdict*, Bodley Head 1984
Wyndham-Browne, W.F., *The Trial of William Herbert Wallace*, Gollancz 1933

6. Red Stains on the Carpet

PRO, HO 144/20678, 20679
PRO, MEPO 3/793
Notable British Trials series: *Buck Ruxton*, Blundell, R.H. and Wilson, G.H. (eds), Hodge 1937
Barden, Dennis, *Famous Cases of Norman Birkett*, Hale 1963
Glaister, John and Brash, James Couper, *Medico-Legal Aspects of the Ruxton Case*, Livingstone 1937
Hardwick, Michael, Doctors on Trial, Herbert Jenkins 1961
Odell, Robin, *Landmarks in Twentieth Century Murder*, Headline 1995
Ward, Jenny, *Crime Busting – Breakthroughs in Forensic Science*, Blandford 1998

7. One Death Sentence Too Many

PRO, ASSI 52/400, 589
PRO, MEPO 3/2990
Celebrated Trials series: *The Trial of Walter Rowland*, Cecil, H., David & Charles 1975
Eddleston, J.J., *Murderous Manchester*, Breedon Books 1997
Koestler, Arthur, *Reflections on Hanging*, Gollancz 1956

9. Death at the Hospital

PRO, ASSI 52/633
Notable British Trials series: *Peter Griffiths*, Godwin G., (ed.), Hodge 1950

Sterling, Jane, *Famous Northern Crimes, Trials and Criminals*, Hesketh 1983
   [also Maybrick, Smith, Wallace and Ruxton]
Thorwald, Jugen, *Marks of Cain*, Thames & Hudson 1965

10. A POISONOUS COUPLE

PRO, DPP 2/2254
PRO, HO 291/229, 230
Firth, J.B., *A Scientist Turns To Crime*, Kimber 1960
Huggett, Renee and Berry, Paul, *Daughters of Cain*, Geo. Allen & Unwin
   1956
Marjoribanks, Edward, *The Life of Sir Edward Marshall Hall*, Victor
   Gollancz 1919
Rowland, John, *Poisoner in the Dock*, Arco 1960
Wilkes, Roger, *An Infamous Address,* Grafton 1989

GENERAL INTEREST (COVERS ALL THE ABOVE)

Bailey, Brian, *Hangman*, Virgin 1993
Gaute, J.H.H. and Odell, Robin, *The Murderer's Who's Who*, Harrap 1979
Lane, Brian, *The Encyclopedia of Forensic Science*, Headline 1992

NEWSPAPERS AND PERIODICALS

Accrington Observer
Bolton Evening News
Bury Times
Daily Express
Daily Telegraph
John Bull
Lancashire Daily Post
Liverpool Post & Echo
News of the World
Northern Daily Telegraph
Southport Visiter
Sunday Dispatch
West Lancashire Evening Gazette

INDEX

Acarnley, James 96
Addison, John 13, 17
Aigburth 1
Aintree Grand National 1, 5
Allen, Harry 129
Allen, Sidney Scholfield 63
Alphon, Peter 106
Anderson, Ethel 79
Anderson, Herbert 79
Anfield Harriers 62
Angood, William 97
arsenic, consumption of 3, 4, 11, 17
Avory, Mr Justice 34, 36, 37

Bailey, Dr Gilbert 123
Baker, George 47
Balchin, Olive 96–9, 101–4
Barnes, Chief Constable Harry 135
Barton, Inspector William 124, 125
Battlecrease House 1, 4, 19
Baxendale, Inspector 12
Beattie, Bernard 80
Beattie, Samuel 57, 58, 63, 64
Berry, James 29
Billing, Dr 44, 45
Bingham, Edith Agnes 30–7
Bingham, Elizabeth 30
Bingham, Gertrude Annie 30, 31, 33
Bingham, James Henry 30–3, 36, 37
Bingham, Margaret 31, 34, 36, 37
Bingham, Nellie 30, 31, 33, 35
Bingham, William Edward Jnr 30
Bingham, William Hodgson 30, 34, 36
Birkett, Norman 88, 91
Black, Chief Constable William 83
Bolton, coroner 113

Brash, Dr James 83, 86
Bremner, Constable 23, 24
Brennan, James Joseph 118
Brewer, Jessie 134, 135
Brierley, Alfred 5, 6, 8, 12, 13, 17
Briggs, Matilda 8, 11, 12
Brindley, David 134
Brisby, Dr Francis Herbert 128
Brown, Dr Andrew 111, 113
Bryning, Superintendent 12
Budd, John 138
Burke, Kenneth 99
Burke, Sarah Kathleen 109
Burnham, Alice 38–44, 46
Burnham, Charles 41, 42, 47
Burnham, Mrs 45, 46, 47,
Bury 20

Cadwallader, Mary 16
Caird, James 63, 68
Callery, Nurse 8, 10
Capstick, Inspector Jack 123–5, 129
Carr, Robert 68
Carter, Dr William 8, 10–12, 14
Cawton, Alice 138
Central Chess Club 57
Chandler, Florence Elizabeth 1–2
City Café 57, 62
Clarenden, Ursula 114
Clark, Inspector Thomas Dodgson 85
Clements, Amy Victoria 106, 111, 115
Clements, Dr Robert George 107–9,
   111–14, 117
Clements, Ernest 115, 117
Clements, George 115, 117
Clements, Sarah Kathleen 109, 111

Close, Alan 62–5, 72
Copley, Elizabeth 98, 99
Cottam, Margaret Crookhall 30, 33
Cottam, Matthew Henry 32
Cox-Walker, Mary 32
Crewe, Joseph 59, 68, 72
Crippen, Hawley Harvey 53
Crossley, Alice 44
Crossley, Joseph 43, 52
Crossley, Margaret 43–5
Curwen, Elizabeth 78, 80, 81

Daily Herald 105
Dalton Square 75
Davies, Edward 13
Devaney, June Anne 122, 123, 127, 129
Draper, Jane Sarah 62
Dukes, William 20, 22–7, 29

East, Norwood 128
Eaton, Arthur Frederick 49
Edge, Rene 121, 127, 128
Edmondson, Robert Blackburn 84
Edmondson, Robert James 78, 80, 85
Egan, Chief Constable Michael 111
Ellis, John 30, 53
Ellison, Joseph 130
Ellwood, Walter Haydn 105
Emerson, Charles 35, 36

Falkner, Sarah Annie 49
Firth, Dr J.B. 101, 105, 114, 138, 139
Flatman's Hotel 5
flypapers, arsenic 6, 8, 10
Forgan, George 134
Fowler's Solution of Arsenic 13, 15
French, Dr 50, 51
Fuller, Dr 14
Fyffe, Maxwell 86

Gardenholme Linn 75, 81
Gardner, Charles Frederick 86, 91
Gayus, Dr Irene 109, 111

Glaister, Professor John 83, 86
Glyn-Jones, Mr Justice 138
Goodman, Jonathan 68, 69, 71
Gordon Furnishing Co. 20
Gordon, George 20–2, 24–7, 29
Gordon, Meyer 20, 23, 24
Gordon, Samuel 20–3
Gore, Ellen Anne 8, 10
Gosling, Wilfred 105
Grace, Dr W.H. 114, 116
Green, Sydney 59
Griffiths, Elizabeth Alice 118
Griffiths, Mary Ellen 118
Griffiths, Pauline 118
Griffiths, Peter Jnr 118–21, 124–9
Griffiths, Peter Snr 118, 128
Grimshaw, Mr 95

Hall, Edward Marshall 52, 53
Hall, Ernest 85
Hampshire, Mary 79, 80, 85, 91
Hanratty, James 106
Hargreaves, John 46
Harley, Gladys 57, 58
Heald, Lionel 138
Heaton, Edwin 4
Hemmerde, Edward 64, 66
Henderson, Superintendent 23
Hewart, Gordon 34, 67, 91
Heywood, Elizabeth 132
Holmes, Dr John 111, 113
Hopwood, Dr J.S. 128
Houston, Dr James Montague 112–17
Hughes, Martha 8, 11
Humphreys, Elizabeth 16
Humphreys, Gwendoline 121–3
Humphreys, Dr Richard 7, 10–14
Huskie, Dr David 83

Jack the Ripper 19
Jackson, J.C. 86, 91
Jannion, Mrs 11
Jenkins, Dr Charles Evans 98

Johnson, Susan Haines 81
Johnston, Mr and Mrs 56, 59, 60, 65
Jolley, J.C. 105

Kershaw, Phillip 88

Lancaster Castle 30
Lee, David 129
Liverpool Daily Post 12, 60
Liverpool FC 54
Lloyd, John 52
Lloyd, Lily 70
Lofty, Margaret Elizabeth 52
Looms, Chief Constable Cornelius G.
  123, 129
Lord Nelson public house 25
Love, George Oliver 47, 48
Lowe, Nora 134

MacDonald, Edward 98, 99, 100
MacFall, Professor John Edward 60, 61,
  63–5, 72, 73
MacIntosh, Dr James Wilson 32
Madden, Eleen 78
Manning, Dr George B. 135, 139
Massey, Francis 36
Mather, Katie 59
Maybrick, Edwin 1, 7–9, 11
Maybrick, Florence Elizabeth 6–9, 11,
  12, 16, 17, 19
Maybrick, Gladys Evelyn 4
Maybrick, James 1, 2, 6, 10–13, 15, 19
Maybrick, James Chandler 4
Maybrick, Michael 1, 7, 8–12, 14, 15
Maybrick, Thomas 7
McCleery, Mary 109
McConnell, W.R. 13
McDougall, Detective Superintendent
  Colin 135
McKeefe, Mary 114
McLellan, Constable 23, 25
Menlove Gardens East 58, 72
Mercer, Norman 98, 99

Mercier, Edyth Anna 109
Merrifield, Alfred 130, 131, 133–5, 137,
  138, 141, 143
Merrifield, Louisa May 130–3, 135–41,
  143
Mighall, Chief Constable Harold 113,
  114
Mitchell, Dr Robert 26
Moore, Superintendent Hubert 61, 66
Mullen, Detective Sergeant 125
Mundy, Bessie 49, 50, 53
Munro, Hector 63, 64, 70

Nahum, Jack de V. 128, 138
Nelson, Jeannie Kerr 78, 84, 85, 88
Newsham, F.A. 128
Nield, Basil 99, 128,

Oliver, Roland 64, 66, 128
Openshaw, H. 99
Oxley, Agnes 78–80, 85

Page, Dr 135
Parkes, John 69, 70, 71
Parkinson, PC Edward 123
Parry, Richard Gordon 68–71, 73, 74
Peel, Sir Robert 20
Pegler, Edith Mabel 48, 49, 51
Phillips, Thomas 58
Pickford, William 13
Pierrepoint, Albert 129, 143
Pierrepoint, Thomas 53
Pinches, Lily 59
Prudential Assurance Co. 54

Qualtrough, R.M. 58, 64

Radio City 71
Reavil, Alice 51
Regan, Bernard 121
Ricketts, Sarah 132, 133–5, 141
Riversdale Road 1
Rogerson, James 81

Rogerson, Jessie 81, 83
Rogerson, Mary Jane 76, 77, 79–81, 85,
    86, 88, 91
Rogerson, Peter 81
Rose, George 49
Ross, Sergeant 23, 24, 25
Ross, Sergeant Thomas James 97
Rothwell, PC James Edward 64
Rowland, Mavis Agnes 94
Rowland, Walter Graham 94–6,
    99–104
Russell, Sir Charles 13, 16
Ruxton, Dr Buck 75, 76, 78–81, 83–6,
    88, 91
Ruxton, Isabella 76–8, 84, 86, 88

Sampson, Annie 32
Sarginson, James 65
Schofield, Annie May 94, 95
Scrutton, Mr Justice 53
Sellers, Mr Justice 99
Serjeant, PC James 59
Shawcross, Hartley 86
Sillitoe, Chief Constable P.J. 83
Singleton, Mr Justice 86
Slinger, Edwin 86
Smalley, Mrs 81, 84
Smith, George Joseph 38–48, 50–3
Smith, George Thomas 47
Smith, Jack Quentin 129
Smith, Mabel 80
Somerville, Henry 105
Southport Visiter 107, 109, 115, 117
Spilsbury, Bernard 53
St George's Hall, Liverpool 13, 64
Stansell, Thomas 17
Stephen, Sir James F. 13, 17, 19
Stevenson, Dr Thomas 14
Stewart, Jack 143

Sunday Graphic and Sunday News 83,
    84
Swift, Thomas 13

Thompson, Arthur 58
Thornhill, Caroline Beatrice 47, 48
Tidy, Dr Charles Meymott 16, 17

Valentine's Meat Juice 7, 10, 11, 16
Valiant, Sergeant Robert 45
Van Ess, Isabella 76
Vann, Chief Constable Henry J. 85, 86
von Roques, Caroline 2

Wallace, Amy 62, 63
Wallace, Julia 56, 60–3, 71, 73
Wallace, William Herbert 54, 57–66, 68,
    70–4
Ware, David John 104–6
Webster, Professor J.N. 139
West Lancs Evening Gazette 132
Weston, Richard 130
Whitfield, Inspector John 34
Whittaker, Loveday 132
Whittington-Egan, Richard 71
Wilcox, William Henry 53
Wildman, James Allison 63
Wilkes, Roger 71
Williams, Henry John 47, 49
Wingate-Saul, Basil 35, 99
Wokes, Thomas S. 6
Wolverton Street, Anfield 54
Wood, Dr Albert 135
Wright, Elsie 62
Wright, Mr Justice 64
Wright, Roland 139

Yapp, Alice 6, 8, 9, 11, 13
Yule, Dr 133, 134